M

Research Paper Handbook

2nd Edition

James D. Lester, Jr.

James D. Lester, Sr.

GOOD YEAR BOOKS

Pearson Learning Group

The following people have contributed to the development of this product:
Art and Design: M. Jane Heelan, Liz Nemeth
Editorial: Monica Glina
Manufacturing: Mark Cirillo, Thomas Dunne
Production: Karen Edmonds, Alia Lesser
Publishing Operations: Carolyn Coyle

ISBN 0-673-61734-3

Printed in the United States of America

1 2 3 4 5 6 7 8 9   06 05 04 03 02 01

This Book Is Printed
on Recycled Paper

1-800-321-3106
www.pearsonlearning.com

Contents

CHAPTER 1

Establishing a Topic

Begin your research project by understanding the assignment and your purpose for the research project. Next, establish a well-focused subject. Your topic may focus on any subject—sports, fashion, or President Theodore Roosevelt. Choose a topic that is interesting to you. It might be a topic that you have always wanted to learn more about, a question that you want answers to, or an investigation into an area that is entirely new. In these early stages of the research project, you must remember that the process can often be confusing and may involve many starts and stops as you move toward a practical topic.

1a Identifying Your Role as a Researcher

The first step in the research process is to identify your role as a researcher. Your voice should reflect the investigative nature of your work, so try to display your knowledge. Refer to authorities that you have consulted by quoting them. Provide charts or graphs that you have borrowed from the sources. Your teachers will give you credit for using the sources in your paper. Just be certain that you give in-text citations to the sources to reflect your academic honesty. Your role is to investigate, explain, defend, and argue the issue.

Establishing a purpose

Research papers perform different functions. They explain, analyze, and persuade, and they often do all of these in the same paper. A writer who argues for the use of peer mediation in school to prevent conflicts must also explain the process and analyze the benefits of the program.

You will use the **explanatory purpose** to review and itemize factual information for the reader. One writer defined "scoliosis" and explained its effect on the spinal column. Another writer explained how carbon monoxide has become a silent killer in our homes.

The **analytical purpose** is used when you classify various parts of the subject in order to investigate each one in depth. One writer examined the effects of cocaine on the brain, the eyes, the lungs, and the heart. Another writer classified and examined the religious symbolism of building the ziggurat, a temple-tower, in ancient cultures.

The **persuasive purpose** addresses the readers with a message of conviction that defends a position. One writer condemned underage drinking and warned of its dangers. Another writer argued that advertisers have enticed children into bad habits: eating poorly, smoking cigarettes, drinking alcohol, and committing acts of violence.

Meeting the needs of your audience

You will want to design your research project for an

academic audience, such as your instructor and fellow students. You are addressing interested readers who expect a depth of understanding on your part and evidence of your background reading on the subject. Try to say something worthwhile by approaching the topic with your special point of view.

For example, the topic "latchkey children" can address the children (to tell them to exercise caution), the parents (to warn them to be vigilant in maintaining phone contact), and even the school administrators (to ask them to consider extending the school day to accommodate working parents).

Match the content of the paper with the needs of the readers. Rather than retelling known facts from an encyclopedia, engage them with interesting interpretations of the evidence.

1b   Selecting a Research Topic

Select a topic with a built-in issue so that you can interpret the issue or problem and cite the opinions of outside sources. When you do, you will bring a focus to your project and give yourself a reason for sharing the findings of other experts with your readers. Each of the following topics addresses a problem or raises an issue:

Children and Video Games: A Question of Addiction

This topic raises two questions: Do children get addicted to video games? With what result?

New Trends in Fashion: The Pressure of Being in Style

This topic focuses on a current issue: Can and should changing trends in fashion worry a young person?

The Foreign Policy of President Theodore Roosevelt

This topic addresses a historical issue: How did President Roosevelt develop the United States as a world power in the early 1900s?

Perhaps you will have little or no trouble deciding on a topic. However, if you are not entirely sure of what topic to research, try any of the following approaches: using personal experience, naming subtopics for a general topic, clustering, asking questions about a topic, or conducting a computer search. Remember to avoid merely writing a summary of a person's life, retelling a piece of fiction, or copying an event of history from reference books.

1c Using Personal Experiences for a Topic Discovery

Everyone has special interests. One of three techniques can spark your interest and perhaps help you discover a subject for your research project:

◆ Combine a personal interest with some point covered in one of your classes: "Basketball and Personal Fitness," or "Television and History."

◆ Consider your future goals and personal beliefs: "Helping Others Learn to Help Themselves: Becoming a Counselor," or "A Recycling Plan for My Home."

◆ Let your cultural background prompt you toward detailed research into your family history, your culture, and the literature and history of your ethnic background: "Hispanic Americans: A Growing Political Force," or "The Decline of the Midwestern Family Farm."

 Exercise 1.1 Write down at least one idea for each of the following topics:

My favorite activity

My favorite school subject

My future goals

My cultural heritage

1d   Exploring Possible Subtopics

Start with a general idea and explore possible subtopics. Perhaps one item on the list can become your research topic. For example, start with biology lab and list subtopics, such as safety, waste disposal, and proper equipment. One of the subtopics might stimulate your thinking about a topic with a built-in issue: "Biology labs need up-to-date equipment, especially to sterilize tools and to protect students."

Exercise 1.2 The seven general categories in this exercise are followed by three subtopics. For each of the seven general headings, write two additional subtopics that interest you.

1. education

yearlong school calendar

computers in school
teaching by television

2. **history**

Rosa Parks
Inventions of Alexander Graham Bell
British Royalty

3. **sociology**

day care centers
street gangs
teenagers as parents

4. **medicine**

a career in nursing
treating teenage drug abuse
rising insurance costs

5. **literature**

The Poetry of Robert Frost
Eudora Welty's "Why I Live at the P.O."
S.E. Hinton's *That Was Then, This Is Now*

6. **popular culture**

rock music lyrics
movie ratings and teen viewers
video games

7. **nature**

neighborhood recycling programs
toxic chemicals vs. clean water
allergic reactions to stinging insects

1e   Clustering Ideas

Some researchers begin with a general idea and cluster ideas around it. Sometimes this clustering technique is known as "creating a web."

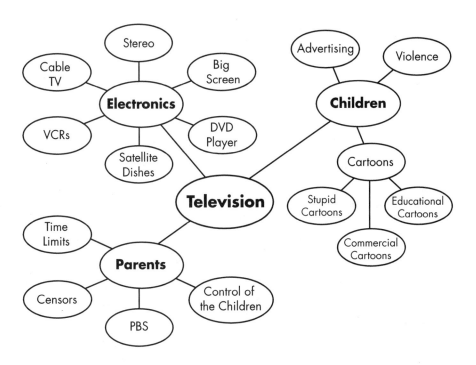

Television

electronics	children	parents
satellite dishes	advertising	censors
VCRs	violence	time limits
cable TV	cartoons	control of the children
stereo	stupid	
big screen	commercial	PBS
DVD player	educational	

Exercise 1.3 Try your skill at clustering. Draw a central balloon on a separate sheet of paper. Write your preliminary topic inside the central balloon. Then, begin filling the connecting balloons. Add more balloons as necessary.

1f   Asking Questions about a General Topic

A question can serve two important purposes. It can address a specific issue or problem that you may wish to investigate. It can also provoke an answer and thereby produce a possible thesis statement. In either case, asking questions will bring a focus to your entire project by narrowing the scope of your research. Here are a few examples of good research questions:

> Do immigrants today face the same kinds of prejudice faced by immigrants 100 years ago?

This topic poses a research issue and will require the writer to define prejudice and cite evidence from source materials.

> What has happened to the Seven Wonders of the Ancient World?

This topic will require the writer to examine the historical facts and the opinions of archeological experts.

> Do some parents spoil little league sports for the girls and boys who participate?

This topic has a built-in bias (the writer has seemingly reached a conclusion), yet it offers a chance for the writer to explore a sensitive issue.

Exercise 1.4 Listed below are sample research questions. For each one, decide if 1) the topic is well-focused and limited, 2) the topic raises an issue or presents a problem worthy of examination, and 3) the topic invites research into outside sources.

1. How does participation in the Boy Scouts and Girl Scouts contribute to the growth of young people?

2. What is *acid rain?*

3. What prompted the older brother to mistreat Doodle in James Hurst's "The Scarlet Ibis"?

4. Are dress codes really necessary in our schools?

5. Why and how did Alaska become a state?

6. Why must American drivers continue to depend on foreign oil?

7. Do rules and regulations in our schools smother creativity in students?

8. What role does television play in the language development of pre-school children?

9. What rights did Helen Keller obtain for persons with physical handicaps?

10. What is the *standard* for standardized tests? Who are students being judged against? Why?

1g Conducting a Computer Search

The Internet, CD-ROMs, and your library's electronic book catalog can quickly show you what research has been done on a topic and even lead you to think about your subject in new ways.

♦ Use a **subject directory** to move from a general subject to a specific topic. The subject directories are hierarchical, so with each mouse click you narrow the topic to a more specific subject.

♦ Use a **key-word search** when you have a specific topic. For example, entering "Martin Luther King, Jr. + Birmingham + demonstration" into a search engine will produce a page with links to several articles on the Birmingham bus boycott, nonviolent demonstrations, and the beginning of the Civil Rights Movement.

Remember to write all pertinent information when you visit a site on the World Wide Web. The URL address is needed to properly document the source in your paper.

Use electronic databases to narrow a topic

Most school and public libraries now have electronic databases, such as *InfoTrac, EBSCOhost, Silverplatter,* or *UMI-Proquest.* These database files refer you to thousands of magazine and journal articles that have been either peer reviewed by experts in the academic field or filtered through magazine and newspaper editorial processes. They take you to more scholarly articles because of the monitoring process as opposed to a general search engine that has multiple key words. In many cases, you can read an abstract of the article and, on occasion, print the entire article. Many databases are now on the Internet; thus, libraries will vary in their holdings, so be sure to check with a reference librarian. Follow these steps:

1. **Select a database.** Some databases, such as *InfoTrac* are general. Other databases, such as *PSYCINFO* (psychological sources) and *ERIC* (educational sources), focus on articles within the discipline.

2. **List key words or a phrase that describes your topic.** For example, the two-word search "teenager embarrassment" will produce several sites that can be easily examined. Below is an example of one source:

   "Do You Embarrass Her?" By: Lynch, Amy; *Daughters,* Jan. 2001, Vol. 6 / Issue 1, 2p *Full Text.*

3. **Examine relevant articles and browse the descriptions.** The entry listed above displays two pages from *Daughters,* a magazine. Hence, the article can be read in full or printed for later study.

Search the electronic book catalog to narrow a subject

Libraries now have computerized indexes to their holdings. Called different names at each library, it is a computer terminal that indexes all books, film strips, video tapes, and sometimes articles in magazines and journals. Like the electronic databases to articles, it will identify specific books that pertain to your topic. Follow these steps:

1. Enter a general subject: religious cults

2. Examine the various subtopics:
   1 – debate and skepticism
   2 – ancient religions
   3 – agnosticism, atheism, and deism

3. Select one topic, perhaps *ancient Egypt,* and you will get a list of books housed in your library.
   1 – *Valley of the Golden Mummies* (2000)
   2 – *Ancient Egypt: The Great Discoveries* (2000)
   3 – *Guide to the Pyramids of Egypt* (1997)

Hint: If the search lists 50 or 60 books for your subject, the topic is too broad and should be narrowed. If it provides only one book, you will need to broaden the topic.

Use individual CD-ROM disks

Browsing in an encyclopedia on CD-ROM will give you a good feel for the depth and strength of the subject and a list of likely topics. For general information, consult an encyclopedia on an individual disk, such as *Encarta* or *Electronic Classical Library.* For specific information, you might try a discipline-related CD, such as the *Oxford English Dictionary.*

Exercise 1.5 For each general subject in this exercise, conduct a computer search using the specific search tool recommended. Be sure to include author names, titles, URL addresses, and any other bibliographic information.

Internet search (URL required):

movie rating system
single parent + daycare

Electronic database such as ProQuest or EbscoHost:

grizzly bear
Amazon rainforest

Electronic book catalog (call number required):

Louis L'Amour
fossil collecting

1h Developing a Thesis Statement

A thesis statement changes your topic or research question into an assertion that you will support with your research. It presents a problem that you will examine with your evidence. The thesis statement must go beyond simply stating the obvious. For example, the following sentence is too simplistic:

Too much television is harmful to children.

This sentence will not engage your readers because they know that excess in anything is harmful. Instead, you should create a thesis statement that is well-focused, raises an issue, and invites research.

Violence in television cartoons can affect children.

The thesis now raises an issue. The writer must research violence on television (particularly in cartoons), report the findings, and explain the effects of television violence on children.

Exercise 1.6 Decide which statements in this exercise assert an idea that will need investigation by the writer and will require the citation of sources in the research paper.

1. Participation in a team sport gives a girl or boy the chance to wear a nice uniform.

2. Acid rain has caused widespread environmental damage in the heavily industrialized areas of the United States.

3. The older brother in James Hurst's "The Scarlet Ibis," mistreats Doodle because he was embarrassed about having "a brother who might not be all there."

4. Dress codes in school have no effect on what students learn.

5. Alaska entered the Union on January 3, 1959, as the 49th state.

6. Automakers resist any changes in the internal combustion engine, so our dependence on foreign oil will continue well into the new century.

7. Individuality is smothered by teachers who expect every student to conform to one standard of learning.

8. English must remain the standard language in all academic classes in the United States.

9. Helen Keller was a pioneer who opened doors for all physically handicapped citizens.

10. Standardized tests cannot judge individual talent.

Use your thesis statement to control and focus the entire paper and to tell the readers the point of your research.

You may change your working thesis at any time during the research because the evidence may lead you to new and different issues. However, your final thesis should meet several criteria. Use the following checklist to evaluate your thesis.

Thesis Checklist

- It expresses your position in a full, declarative sentence that is not a question, not a statement of purpose, and not merely a topic.

- It limits the subject to one issue that has grown out of research.

- It establishes an investigative, inventive edge to your research and thereby gives a reason for all your work.

- It points forward to the conclusion.

- It prompts you to seek evidence in the library.

If you have trouble discovering your thesis at first, ask yourself a few questions. The answer might very well be the thesis:

1. What is the point of my research?

   Recent research demonstrates that self-guilt often causes a teenager to have emotional problems.

2. What do I want this paper to prove?

   Student clubs need school funding. Students should not be required to sell products to raise funds.

3. Can I tell the reader anything new or different?

   Evidence indicates that advertisers have bought their way into the classroom with free educational materials.

4. Do I have a solution to the problem?

   Public support for "safe" houses will provide a haven for children abused by their parents.

5. Do I have a new approach to the issue?

Personal economics is a force to be reckoned with, and poverty, not greed, forces many youngsters into a life of crime.

6. Should I take a less popular view of this matter?

African-American voters have proved to be a powerful political force at election time.

7. What exactly is my theory about this subject?

Trustworthy employees, not mechanical safeguards on hardware and software, will prevent theft of software, sabotage of mainframes, and damaging viruses in computer systems.

Exercise 1.7 Listed in this exercise are five thesis statements. For each statement, write a question that each one answers. Example:

Thesis: Research papers stimulate the mind.

Question: What purpose is served by completing research projects?

1. Recyling paper, plastic, and glass is justified for environmental reasons.

2. Public school athletic programs promote school and public pride.

3. Jogging damages a person's knees, ankles, and feet.

4. Schools should convert to a yearlong calendar.

5. Respect is the most important ingredient in human relationships.

1i   Framing a Research Proposal

You may need to write a research proposal and have it approved by your instructor before beginning research in a library. The research proposal will give your work direction so that both your teacher and the school media specialist can serve your specific needs.

Research Proposal Checklist

A research proposal is a short paragraph that identifies the essential ingredients of your work:

- The purpose of the paper

- The intended audience

- Your role as a research writer

- The thesis statement

One student writer developed this research proposal:

> It saddens me to see people, even children, throwing away their lives on cocaine addiction. My role is to explain to my schoolmates the effects of cocaine on various organs of the body. I will defend this thesis: Cocaine will not make you anything except dead, or almost dead.

This writer identifies herself as a protester (*role*) against the use of cocaine (*purpose*). She will argue her idea (*thesis*) to her schoolmates (*audience*).

1j Expressing a Thesis Statement in the Proposal

Your preliminary thesis is an important part of the proposal because it sets in motion your examination of facts that point to a conclusion. Your thesis will show the special nature of your paper. Note how four students arrived at different thesis statements even though they had the same topic, "Santiago in Hemingway's *The Old Man and the Sea.*"

Note: The novel narrates the toils of an old Cuban fisherman named Santiago who has not caught a fish for many days. He desperately needs the money to be gained by returning with a good catch of fish. On this day, he catches a marlin that pulls him far out to sea. Finally, Santiago ties the huge marlin to the side of his boat. However, during the return in the darkness, sharks attack the marlin so that Santiago arrives home with only a skeleton of the fish.

This writer will examine Santiago's economic condition.

> **Thesis:** Poverty forced Santiago to venture too far and struggle beyond his strength in his attempt to catch the giant fish.

This writer will look at the religious and social symbolism of the novel.

> **Thesis:** The giant marlin is a symbol for all of life's obstacles and hurdles, and Santiago is a symbol for all suffering humans.

This writer will explore the history of fishing equipment and explain Santiago's failure.

> **Thesis:** Santiago represents a dying breed, the person

who confronts the natural elements alone, without modern technology.

This writer takes a social approach to examine the Cuban culture and its influence on Hemingway.

Thesis: Hemingway's portrayal of Santiago demonstrates the author's deep respect for Cubans and Cuba, where he lived for many years.

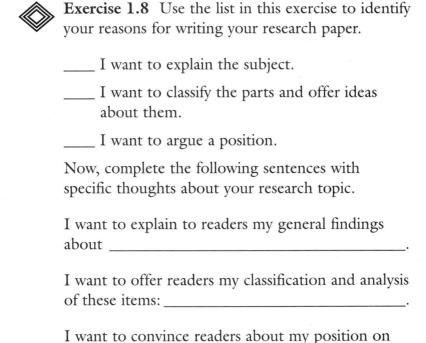

Exercise 1.8 Use the list in this exercise to identify your reasons for writing your research paper.

_____ I want to explain the subject.

_____ I want to classify the parts and offer ideas about them.

_____ I want to argue a position.

Now, complete the following sentences with specific thoughts about your research topic.

I want to explain to readers my general findings about _____.

I want to offer readers my classification and analysis of these items: _____.

I want to convince readers about my position on

_____.

Exercise 1.9 Before writing your own proposal, study the following two research proposals. Identify the purpose, writer's role, audience, and thesis in each.

I want to investigate the life of Mahatma Gandhi in order to explain his role in establishing India's independence and to list the reasons for his mission in life. I want to endorse his overwhelming commitment to nonviolent change.

I want art students to understand that Leonardo da Vinci was one of the greatest painters of the Renaissance. My job is to defend Leonardo da Vinci and argue that his genius contributed to art, science, literature, religion, and engineering.

On a separate sheet of paper, write your research proposal and submit it to your teacher for approval.

CHAPTER 2

Gathering Data

With a refined topic in hand, you can begin research in your school's media center, on the Internet, and in the community. After your teacher approves your research proposal, you can begin your search for the best sources. Be sure to cite all information about a source in a working bibliography. Remember that a well-written research paper will include many adjustments and modifications as you begin to gather data.

Steps in the research process

Search the available sources. Access the Electronic Book Catalog of reference books, bibliographies, and indexes in your school's media center, then turn to available computer sources such as the Internet and CD-ROM programs. This step shows the availability of source materials and provides a beginning set of references.

Refine the topic and evaluate the sources. Spend time skimming articles, comparing sources, and reading through important sections of books to narrow your topic to a purpose that you believe will be manageable. Your source information should include a mix of journal articles, books, Internet articles, and possibly field research.

Take shortcuts. Look for reference sources by discipline. For example, if your topic deals with schools or an issue in education, go online to search *ERIC* or *Edweb*. Secondly, use the electronic book catalog in your school's media center as well as electronic services such as *Infotrac* and *Silverplatter*.

Read and take notes. Draw ideas and quotations from books, essays, articles, computer printouts, and government documents. Write complete notes as you read so that you can write them into your text. Do not delay the writing task or you will face a huge, imposing pile of information.

Your task is not simply to find sources. You must select the most appropriate selections from the sources and incorporate them into the framework of your ideas about the subject.

2a Developing a Working Bibliography

A working bibliography is a list of the sources that you plan to consult before drafting your paper. Too few sources about your topic can signal that your topic is too narrow or obscure. Too many sources indicates that you need a tighter focus. A set of bibliographic entries has three purposes:

◆ It locates books and articles for note-taking purposes.

◆ It provides information for the in-text citations, as in the following example in MLA style:

> "The numerous instances of stalking in Internet chat rooms has been noted by Hargrove (37–39) and Whitmire (216)."

◆ It provides information for the final reference page. Therefore, preserve all computer printouts and handwritten notes.

Whether you keyboard your sources or make handwritten notes, each entry in your working bibliography should contain the following information, with variations, of course, for books, periodicals, and government documents:

1. Author's name

2. Title of the work

3. Publication information

4. Library call number

5. URL address from the Internet

6. A personal note about the contents of the source

For other types of entries, such as an anthology, a lecture, or a map, consult the Index of this book, which will direct you to appropriate pages for samples of almost every imaginable type of bibliographic entry. Use the same format in your working bibliography that you will need for your finished manuscript.

Bibliographic entry for a book (MLA style):

DS554.8/ P39 / 2001

Partridge, Larry. *Flying Tigers over Cambodia: An American Pilot's Memoir of the 1975 Phnom Penh Airlift.* Jefferson, NC: McFarland, 2001.

Bibliographic entry for a journal article (MLA style):

Ziskind, Esther S. "The Social Context of Nonverbal Behavior." *American Journal of Psychiatry* 158 (2001): 150-56.

Bibliographic entry for a magazine (MLA style):

Wiley, John P. "Serpent Surprise." *Smithsonian* Apr. 2001: 92–95.

Bibliographic entry for an Internet article (MLA style):

Macleod, Scott. "The King of Cool." *Time.Com Magazine*
26 June 2000. 18 April, 2001. <http://www.time.com/
time/magazine/articles/0,3266,47707,00.html>.

2b Conducting a Key-Word Search

When you know your topic, perform a key-word
search using the words you would like to find in
the title, description, or text of a source. For
example, to find information on Theodore
Roosevelt's formation of the Bull Moose Party, you
would enter the words *Bull* and *Moose* and *Theodore
Roosevelt*. An Internet search engine will direct you
to a list of sites:

> http://gi.grolier.com/presidents/aae/side/
> bullmoos.html
> http://www.let.rug.nl/~usa/volun/
> bullmoos.htm.

You can then read the articles to determine if they
relate to your research efforts. Search engines
usually put the most relevant or most popular
sites first, so the first five to ten sites listed will be
likely sources.

It is extremely important for you to give readers
clear documentation to the sources that are cited in
your paper. This need for honesty and integrity
requires accurate records and a close evaluation of
each source for its scholarly value. (See pages
32–33 for guidelines on evaluating online sources.)

Tips for key-word searching

1. If you type a single word (i.e., *brain*), you often

will get a long list of sites containing the term, most having little relevance to your topic. Generally, it is better to search with more than one word. Lowercase words will also find capitalized words. For example, *brain* will find brain, Brain, and BRAIN.

2. If you provide two or more words with *and* between each one, the search engine will find only sources that combine all words: brain *and* injury *and* accidents.

3. Attach a "+" in front of words that must appear in documents and a "–" in front of words that *must not* appear: brain + injury – tumor. This request will give you documents that mention the *brain* and *injury* but will eliminate any documents that include the word *tumor.*

4. You may also use *not* to eliminate a term: brain *and* injury *not* tumor. This request will focus the search on sites relative to the brain and brain injuries but not brain tumors.

5. Use quotation marks around two words to make them one unit, although proper names do not need quotation marks: "brain injury." This request will give you documents that combine both brain and injury. The use of phrases is perhaps the best way to limit the number of hits by the search engine.

A key-word search involves several steps. For example, one writer went in search of sources on the topic "Acne." He focused on creams, drugs, and other medications. He began his pursuit of credible sources by contemplating such questions as these:

1. What title best describes my paper's content?

2. What are the specific topics, synonyms, closely related phrases, and alternate spellings of my subject, using scientific, technical, and common names?

3. What related topics should be excluded to narrow my search?

4. Should citations be limited to a specific publication year(s)?

The purpose of this questionnaire should be fairly obvious: the researcher needs terminology to feed into the key-word source. Usually, three key terms are needed to control a search of the sources: **ACNE + DRUGS + THERAPY.**

The computer will browse through records to select only those items that match books and articles related to each of the three terms. The computer will then produce a list of Internet sites and sources on the topic. The following entries were found after a key-word search on *altavista.com*. (Internet sites are likely to change, so you may encounter sites that are no longer active.)

Key Word Search: Acne + Drugs + Therapy

Widemark, Sue. "Drug, Accutane (for Acne) causes nasty possibly permanent problems." *FDA Consumer's Magazine* June 1998. 18 Feb. 2001 <http://www.cin.org/archives/cinhealth/199806/00039.html>.

"Acne." Altruis Miomedical Network. 18 Feb. 2001 <http://www.acne-drug.com>.

Johnson, Betty A., M.D. and Julia R. Nunley, M.D. "Topical Therapy for Acne Vulgaris." *Postgraduate Medicine* 107.3 March 2000. 19 Feb. 2001 <http://www.postgradmed.com/issues/2000/03_00/johnson.htm>.

These Internet sites and many others listed in the

key-word search will provide information about the use of drug therapy in the prevention of acne. Make a printout of any important data and the source information for each source.

Many teachers like for their students to keep a set of bibliography cards; however, a system that is just as effective is to designate a set of notebook pages for recording bibliographic information. Using notebook sheets allows more room for you to write notes and comments concerning the source. Whether you keep a set of bibliography note cards or notebook pages, be sure to include all pertinent source information for the citation.

 Exercise 2.1 Write a bibliographic entry for the following source from a CD-ROM terminal:

Bacterial Resistance in Acne by E.A. Eady v196.1
 Dermatology 1998, p59–66.

Exercise 2.2 Write a bibliographic entry based on information found in the following entry from the Internet:

<http://www.ebody.com/dermatology/acne_treatments.html>
 "Acne Treatments." EBody.com February 3, 2001.

2c Searching the Electronic Book Catalog

The Electronic Book Catalog in your school's media center lists all books in your media center by title, by last name of the author, and by subject. Begin your search at the computer terminal by conducting a key-word search, such as "TELEVISION and CHILDREN," which will list a number of books. The next procedure is to record all information into a working bibliographic entry. (See Chapter 10, "Works Cited," for ways to write the various bibliographic forms.)

Keyword Search Request: Television and children
Bibliographic record No. 3 of 3 entries found

Macklin, M. Carole & Les Carlson, eds.
    Advertising to Children: Concepts and Controversies /
    M. Carole Macklin (Editor), Les Carlson (Editor).
    Thousand Oaks, CA: Sage Publications, 1999. 322
    pp.; Includes index.

SUBJECT HEADINGS
    Television Advertising and Children
    Advertising and Children

LOCATION: Main library

CALL NUMBER: MC1882.8 C45 P33

Include the following pieces of information for your bibliographic entry: 1) call number, 2) author, 3) title, 4) place of publication, 5) publisher, 6) date, 7) note on the book's contents.

Bibliographic entry for a book (MLA style):
MC1882.8/C45/P33
    Macklin, M. Carole and Les Carlson, eds. *Advertising*
    to Children: Concepts and Controversies. Thousand
    Oaks, CA: Sage, 1999.

Exercise 2.3 Write a bibliographic entry based on information found in the following entry from the Library's Electronic Network. Remember to list call number, author, title, editor, edition, place, publisher, and year.

Anijar, Karen
    Teaching Toward the 24th Century: Star Trek as Social
    Curriculum.
    New York: Falmer Press, 2000.

Bibliography p. 235–54; includes index
xiv, 265 p.: ill.; 23 cm

SUBJECT HEADINGS:
Critical pedagogy — United States
Curriculum change — United States
Popular culture — United States

LOCATION: General Stacks

CALL NUMBER: LC196.5 .U6 A56

Always be sure to record the complete **library call number**. Writing the correct form now will save a lot of time when you work to complete the manuscript. Your media center will classify its books by one of two systems, the Library of Congress (LC) system or the Dewey Decimal System. Most high school media centers use the Dewey Decimal call number system. Most college libraries use the Library of Congress call numbers. A public access catalog entry usually features both sets of numbers.

The next example shows the differences in the systems:

Library of Congress:	**Dewey Decimal:**
HQ [Social Sciences]	327.56 [Political Science]
1236 [Politics]	.M35 [Author Number]
.M347 [Author Number]	

By using either set of numbers, depending upon your media center, you should find this book:

Martin, Mart. *The Almanac of Women and Minorities in World Politics.* Boulder, CO: Westview, 2000.

Exercise 2.4 With the help of your teacher or a media specialist, begin using the Electronic Book Catalog to discover the availability of books, articles, and resources pertaining to your research topic. Use the computer to gather at least three pieces of data.

2d Searching a Library's Electronic Databases

On your school's library network you will have access to electronic databases such as *InfoTrac, Silverplatter, ProQuest,* and others. These databases will guide you to several sources, provide an abstract of the article, and then provide a full-text version of the article.

Bibliographic entry for a journal article (MLA style):

Finch, Robert. "On the Killing Fields." *The Georgia Review* 54 (2000): 132.

Bibliographic entry for a magazine (MLA style):

Kline, Robert M. "Whose Blood Is It Anyway?" *Scientific American* Apr. 2001: 42–49.

In addition to electronic databases, the H.W. Wilson Company has provided printed indexes to periodical literature for many years. The company has kept current by now providing its indexes online. It catalogs articles in a wide variety of periodicals in many disciplines.

Readers' Guide to Periodical Literature indexes reading for the early stages of research in magazines, such as:

Astronomy	*Physics Today*
Business Week	*Psychology Today*
Earth Science	*Science Digest*
Foreign Affairs	*Technology Review*
Health	

Social Sciences Index indexes journal articles for periodicals in fields, such as economics, geography, political science, psychology, and medical science.

Humanities Index catalogs over 250 publications in fields such as archaeology, performing arts, history, language and literature, and religion.

Applied Science and Technology Index provides articles in chemistry, engineering, computer science, mathematics, physics, and related fields.

Biological and Agricultural Index lists articles in biology, zoology, botany, agriculture, and related fields.

Education Index presents articles in education, physical education, and related fields.

Business Periodicals Index lists business, marketing, advertising, and related articles in the business field.

 Exercise 2.5 Write a bibliographic entry for the following source from a CD-ROM terminal:

Bacterial Resistance in Acne by E.A. Eady v196.1
    Dermatology 1998, p59–66.

2e   Searching the Internet

The **Internet,** a worldwide computer network, offers instant access to hundreds of thousands of computer files relating to almost any subject across the curriculum, including articles, illustrations, sound and video clips, and raw data, making it a huge library of source materials. The easiest entry to this network, most researchers find, is the **World Wide Web,** which is a set of specially linked computer files or "web sites"—including articles, images, or programs. You can access the Web by means of special software called a browser. The most common browsers are *Netscape Navigator* and *Microsoft Internet Explorer.*

Bibliographic entry for an Internet article (MLA style):

Reuben, Paul P. "Chapter 4: Early Ninteenth Century: Walt Whitman (1819–1892)." 13 June 1999. 11 Sept. 2001 <http://www.csustan.edu/english/reuben/pal/chap4/whitman_sfcreview.html>.

The connections between web sites appear as **hypertext links.** Links are *hot* text or icons that, when clicked, instruct the computer to perform certain functions, such as to go to another file within the vast web network. You will know that text is hot when it is underlined and appears in a color unlike that of the rest of the text or when the cursor changes to a hand.

You have several options when you load a browser, like Netscape, and its various directories and search engines, such as *Yahoo!, Infoseek, AltaVista,* or *Excite.*

A **subject directory** at *Yahoo!* or other search engines help you conduct a key-word search that indexes a sequence of hierarchical subjects. That is, it moves you from general to specific topics. You might start with *finance,* move to *campaign finance,* then move to *campaign finance reform,* and arrive finally at *public financing of political campaigns.* (See "Conducting a Key-Word Search," page 24.)

Checklist: Evaluating Internet Sources

The Internet supplies huge amounts of material.

Some of it is excellent, and some is not so good. You must make judgments about the validity of these materials. In addition to your common sense judgment, here are a few guidelines:

1. Utilize the *edu* and *org* sites. Usually, these will be domains developed by an educational institution or by a professional organization, such as the American Psychological Association.

2. The *gov* (government) and *mil* (military) sites usually have reliable materials. The *com* (commercial) sites can become suspect for several reasons: 1) they are selling advertising space, 2) they often charge you for access to their files, 3) they can be ISP sites (Internet Service Provider) which people pay to use and to post their material.

3. Look for the *professional* affiliation of the writer, which you will find in the opening credits or in an E-mail address.

4. Look for a bibliography that accompanies the article, which will indicate the scholarly nature of this writer's work.

5. Treat E-mail messages as mail, not scholarly articles.

6. Does the site give you hypertext links to other professional sites or to commercial sites? Links to other educational sites serve as a modern bibliography to more reliable sources. Links to commercial sites can often be attempts to sell you something.

Locating online periodicals

Search out articles on your topic by accessing

online journals, magazines, and newspapers. Many can be found with these directories:

NewsDirectory.Com <http://ecola.com/new/>

Electric Library <http://www.elibrary.com/>

Pathfinder <http://pathfinder.com/>

ZD Net <http://www.zdnet.com/>

After you find a magazine or journal of your choice, make a bookmark so that you can access it quickly. A few sites for newspapers are listed below:

The New York Times <http://www.nytimes.com>

USA Today <http://www.usatoday.com>

U.S. News Online <http://www.usnews.com>

Wall Street Journal <http://www.wsj.com>

Other magazines, journals, and newspapers can be found online by using search engines.

Exercise 2.6 Write a bibliographic entry based on information found in the following entry from the Internet:

> <http://www.ebody.com/dermatology/acne_treatments.html>
> "Acne Treatments." EBody.com February 3, 2001.
> Accessed on September 11, 2001.

2f Searching for an Encyclopedia Article

CD-ROMs are good for 1) obtaining information, 2) searching large sections of text, and 3) copying and pasting text into your manuscript. For general information as you begin your research, consult individual programs, such as *Grolier's Encyclopedia, Encarta,* or *Electronic Classical Library.*

CD-ROMs now make it possible to download selected passages and paste them into your text. You can download biographical and critical articles to your paper, while giving scholarly credit. These loadable diskettes also give you access to research tools, such as the *Oxford English Dictionary, IBM Dictionary of Computing,* or *McGraw-Hill Encyclopedia of World Economies.* Specific diskettes are also available for such titles as: *The History of American Literature, America's Civil War: A Nation Divided,* or *The Best of Herman Melville.* (See pages 10–11 in Chapter 1 for details about CD-ROM databases, such as *InfoTrac* or *Silverplatter.*)

Bibliographic entry for an encyclopedia article on (MLA style):

"Foot-and-Mouth Disease." *Encarta Encyclopedia.* CD-ROM. Microsoft Corporation. 2001.

2g   Searching for a Newspaper Article

Electronic networks now enable you to find newspaper articles from across the nation. Your school media center may have a newspaper search engine on its network, or you may need to go to the Internet and access www.newspapers.com. This resource will take you to entries from over 800 newspapers. In most cases, an online newspaper will have its own internal search engine that enables you to examine articles from its archives.

Bibliographic entry for a newspaper article (MLA style):

Crider, Kitty. "20 Questions About Buying, Cooking, and Handling Meat." *The Atlanta Journal-Constitution* 19 Apr., 2001: H1+.

 Exercise 2.7 Write a bibliographic entry for the following information to an article in the *Chicago Tribune:*

An article by Ruth E. Igoe and Mickey Ciokajlo entitled "Ice-packed Roofs Bring a Winter Water Torture." From the *Chicago Tribune,* Wednesday, January 3, 2001, page A1.

2h Searching for Government Documents

All branches of the government publish massive amounts of material. Investigate government documents through one of two resources:

GPO on Silverplatter on your library's network or

GPOAccess on the Internet

Either of these sites will take you to files of the Government Printing Office. The database list includes *Congressional Bill, Congressional Record, Economic Indicators, Public Laws,* and the *U.S. Constitution.*

Bibliographic entry for a government document (MLA style):

United States. Cong. Senate. *Working Family Tax Relief Act of 2001.* 22 Jan. 2001. 107th Cong. Senate Bill 9. 19 May, 2001 <http://thomas.loc.gov/cgi-bin/query/z?c107: S.9>.

Books found through the electronic book catalog, periodical articles found through a CD-ROM search, or an Internet article found in a key-word search are only part of the resources available for your research project. You might also do some of your research outside the library. Field research will require different kinds of notes that might include charts, laboratory notebooks, or research journals.

If you **interview** knowledgeable people, make careful notes during the interview and transcribe those notes into your draft. A tape recorder can serve as a back-up to your note taking; however, first get permission from the person you are interviewing.

If you conduct a survey using a **questionnaire,** the results will become valuable data for developing notes, graphs, and charts for your research project.

Empirical research, often performed in a laboratory, can determine why and how things exist, function, and interact with one another. This type of project will explain your methods and findings in pursuit of a hypothesis (your thesis). **Experiments, tests,** and **measurements** serve as your notes for the "results" section of the report and will give you the basis for the "discussion" section.

In addition to experimental research, you might watch a television program, attend a lecture, request information by letter, or gather information through e-mail. In every case, you must also prepare a bibliographic entry that indicates the type of source used.

Television, videotape, audiotape. If you borrow ideas from any type of audiovisual material, note carefully the source and cite specific catalog numbers if they are readily available. Below are two examples of bibliographic entries of audiovisual materials:

From Earth to the Moon. Dir. Tom Hanks. Documentary. HBO Video, 1998.

"Women & Fibroids." Narr. Jovita Moore. *Action News.* WATC, Atlanta. 8 Aug. 2000.

Interview, letter, miscellaneous unpublished sources. If you interview somebody and plan to use their words and ideas in your paper, write a bibliographic entry that lists the person, the type of information (letter, private papers, photocopied material), the place, and the date. If you think it is appropriate, add other pertinent information, such as, "Jackson, John, county historian" or "Lamkin, Mabel. Correspondence with Governor Pike."

Kraak, Phillip. Telephone interview. 18 Jan. 2001.

Noell, Shannon. Letter to the author. 5 Mar. 2001.

 Exercise 2.8 Write a bibliographic entry for each of the following:

1. An article entitled "Eastwood, Clint" that appears in alphabetical order in *Current Biography Yearbook,* published in 2001.

2. "News Special," *CBS News,* CBS-TV, 5 April 2001.

3. A personal letter addressed to you from Montgomery, Alabama, from Ellen W. Grissom, dated March 10, 2001.

CHAPTER 3

Setting Goals and Organizing Ideas

After your initial search for source materials, you need to organize your ideas so that reading and note taking will relate directly to your specific needs. Despite careful planning, developing a paper is usually haphazard, at best, with bits of information scattered everywhere and in different forms, such as notes, photocopied material, and printouts from the Internet.

Your notes must grow from carefully drawn plans, which may include a research proposal, a list of ideas or questions, or a rough outline. If you are working with an assigned topic, you may not have developed your own angle for the subject yet. You will find your own way through the maze, and the organizational ideas that follow will serve your needs.

Suppose, for example, that you wish to examine an event from U.S. history, such as the Spanish-American War. Four academic disciplines will approach the same topic in the different ways shown on the next page:

Political Science. The political ambitions of Theodore Roosevelt may have propelled his "Rough Riders" into danger with the charge up San Juan Hill.

Economics. The push for Cuban independence occurred, in part, because of a spirit of imperialism growing in the United States—fueled by supporters of Manifest Destiny—to seek development that would enrich our own nation.

Military Science. The sinking of the battleship *Maine* on the night of February 15 resulted in the national battle cry, "Remember the *Maine!*"

Geography. The close proximity of Cuba to the United States mainland made the Spanish-American War strategically important.

3a Charting a Direction and Setting Goals

Do not plunge too quickly into note taking. You need to know *what* to look for and *why* you need it. Frame your key ideas in the form of a proposal, list, or outline.

Your **research proposal** (see page 17) outlines issues that you will need to investigate. For example, the last sentence of the following research proposal names two topics worthy of research.

> The purpose of my study is to examine the negative and positive effects of television viewing on the language development of children. My goal is to examine, classify, and discuss the situation. I may need to warn parents and teachers of certain dangers, I may need to explain how to use television effectively, or I may need to do both.

A list of **key words** and **phrases** focuses your research using the terms most important to your issue. Jot down ideas or words in a rough list and then expand the list to show a hierarchy of major and minor ideas:

educational programming

children's television

vocabulary development

television as babysitter

reading comprehension

language development

The researcher could use these words as the tag lines to begin each note.

A **rough outline** will arrange the words and phrases to focus on the key issues concerning television viewing by children:

Television viewing by children

Vocabulary development

Reading development

Language development

Positive influences of television on children

Educational programming

Learning skills

Negative matters with television and children

Used as a babysitter

Effects on children's eyesight

Psychological damage

This outline, although sketchy, provides the terminology for scanning sources, taking notes, and drafting the paper.

A **list of questions** about your topic will invite you to develop answers in your notes.

Do children benefit from educational programming?

What effect does television have on a child's educational development?

Why do parents use the television as a babysitter?

Can a child's eyesight be affected by prolonged television viewing?

What learning skills can children gather by viewing television?

You should try to answer every question with at least one note, as shown here:

Children's Programming   AAP

The American Academy of Pediatrics recommends that children under two years of age should not watch television at all. The AAP feels that, "too much TV can negatively affect brain development."

Source:
"Is TV Really Bad for Our Children?" American Academy of Pediatrics. 11 Jan. 2000. 16 April 2001 <http://childrenstv.about.com/parenting/childrenstv/library/weekly/aa011100a.htm>.

The **modes of development** can help you build effective paragraphs. One writer developed this list:

Define language development

Compare educational programs

Illustrate television used as a babysitter with several examples

Use **statistics** and **scientific data**

Classify the types of learning development that can occur

Search out **consequences** of prolonged television viewing

Give **narrative** examples

With this information in hand, a writer can search for material to complete **definitions** and supply **examples.** Develop the important items on the list into full paragraphs. Write a paragraph that compares television programs and educational value, or another that gives detailed explanation with illustrations. By doing so, you will be well on your way to developing the project.

A thesis statement will chart the direction of your research project. Below your thesis statement, list concepts that will expand upon the thesis, as shown next:

> **Thesis:** Television can have positive effects on a child's language development.
>
> 1. Television introduces new words.
> 2. Television reinforces word usage and proper syntax.
> 3. Literary classics come alive verbally on TV.
> 4. Television provides the subtle rhythms and musical effects of the best speakers.

The outline above can help the writer produce four positive outcomes of television viewing.

Checklist: Setting a Direction for the Project

- ◆ Write a research proposal for your research project.
- ◆ List key words and phrases.
- ◆ Map out a rough outline for the key points.
- ◆ Speculate by asking questions and finding sources to answer the questions.
- ◆ Build effective paragraphs by using various modes of development.
- ◆ Formulate a thesis that charts the direction of the project.

Exercise 3.1 If you have not already done so, use your research journal to draft a **research proposal** and submit it to your teacher for approval.

Exercise 3.2 For your own research project, develop one of the following preliminary steps before writing your outline. You may want to develop all three.

A. A list of ideas and issues

Subject:

Five major issues:

B. A set of questions to be answered

My investigation will answer why? how? where? what? and how much?

C. An investigative plan

I plan to examine the following three issues:

From these issues, I hope to reach a conclusion about:

Exercise 3.3 Create a rough outline from your list of key words and phrases. Begin by writing your **thesis statement.** Then, give at least **three specific categories** for your topic.

3b   Stimulating Your Note Taking

A paradigm is a plan that provides a general organizational model and basic platform for research projects. The paradigm is an ideal pattern for many different projects and can be an effective way to stimulate note taking. In contrast, an outline is a specific plan for one paper only. Start with a paradigm and finish with an outline.

If you have any hesitation about the design of your paper, start with this skeletal model and expand it with your material. Readers, including your instructor, are accustomed to this sequence for research papers. It offers plenty of leeway.

Identify the subject
   Explain the problem
   Provide background information
   Frame a thesis statement
Analyze the subject
   Examine the first major issue
   Examine the second major issue
   Examine the third major issue
Discuss your findings
   Restate your thesis and point beyond it
   Interpret the findings
   Provide answers, solutions, a final judgment

To the introduction, you can add a quotation or a definition. Within the body, you can compare, analyze, give evidence, trace historical events, and handle many other matters. In the conclusion, you can challenge an assumption, take exception to a prevailing point of view, and reaffirm your thesis.

A model for argument or persuasion research projects

Many teachers prefer for their students to write persuasively or argue from a set position. For this type of research paper, you should conform in general to this next paradigm. Select the elements that fit your design.

Introduction

> A statement that establishes the problem or controversial issue that your paper will examine
>
> A summary of the issues
>
> Definition of key terminology
>
> A concession on some points of the argument
>
> Quotation and paraphrase of sources to build the controversial nature of the subject
>
> Background information to establish past theories and current ideas on the topic
>
> A thesis that establishes your position on the issue

Body

> Arguments in defense of one side
>
> Analysis of the issues, both pro and con
>
> Evidence from the sources, including quotations

Conclusion

> Your thesis expanded into a conclusion that makes clear your position, which should be one that grows logically from your analysis and discussion of the issues

Remember that the formulas provided above are general guidelines, not ironclad rules. Adjust each as necessary to meet your needs.

3c   Writing a Formal Outline

A formal outline categorizes the issues of your study into clear, logical divisions with main headings and one or more levels of subheadings. Not all research projects require the formal outline, nor do some researchers need to use one. A short research project can be created from key words, a list of issues, a rough outline, and a rough draft. After all, the outline and a first draft are preliminary steps to discovering what needs further exploration.

However, many writers benefit by developing a formal outline that categorizes the investigation into clear, logical divisions. The outline will give unity and coherence to your miscellaneous handwritten notes, computer drafts, and photocopied materials. It helps to change miscellaneous notes into an ordered progression of ideas. A formal outline is not rigid and inflexible; you may, and should, modify it while writing and revising.

You may wish to experiment with the outline feature of your word processor. If you use the feature when composing the original document, it will allow you to view the paper at various levels of detail and to "drop" the essay into a different organization.

Using standard outline symbols

List your major categories and sub-topics:

I. First major heading

  A. Subheading of first degree

    1. Subheadings of second degree

    2.

      a. Subheadings of third degree

      b.

        (1) Subheadings of fourth degree

        (2)

          (a) Subheadings of fifth degree

          (b)

  B. Subheading of first degree

Each division must be in two parts. If you have a *I*, you must have a *II*. If you have an *A*, you must have a *B*. The degree to which you continue the subheads will depend, in part, upon the complexity of the subject. Subheads in a research paper seldom carry beyond the first series of small letters.

Writing a formal topic outline

Build a topic outline with balanced phrases. The advantage of the topic outline is the speed with which you can develop it. The following example uses noun phrases:

I. Television's effects on children

  A. Vocabulary development

  B. Reading ability

  C. Visual arts appreciation

  D. Writing efficiency

  E. Discovery of technology

II. Reading's effects on children

The topic outline may also use gerund phrases ("Learning vocabulary" and "Learning to read") or infinitive phrases ("To develop a vocabulary" or "To learn to read").

Writing a formal sentence outline

The sentence outline requires full sentences for each heading and subheading. It has two advantages over the topic outline. First, many entries in a sentence outline can serve as topic sentences for paragraphs, thereby speeding up the writing process. Second, the subject-verb pattern establishes the direction of your thinking. For example, the phrase "Vocabulary development" becomes "Television viewing can improve a child's vocabulary."

A portion of one writer's outline follows.

I. Television talk shows distort the truth.

   A. Talk shows skew objectivity and distort the truth.

      1. The producers and directors contrive an illusion of the truth.

      2. They are guilty of falsifying the line between fact and fiction.

   B. We need to recognize television as a presentation, like a drama.

      1. Social reality is not a staple of television broadcasting.

      2. Viewers who abandon social reality buy into the sales pitch of television producers who promote both the show and the advertised products.

The sentence outline reveals any possible organizational problems rather than hiding them as a topic outline might do. The time devoted to writing a complete sentence outline will benefit you when you write the rough draft and revise it.

It is important to remember that the finished research project should trace the issues, defend and support a thesis, and provide a dynamic progression of issues and concepts that point to the conclusion. Each section of the paper should provide these elements:

◆ Identification of the problem or issue

◆ Analysis of the issues

◆ Presentation of evidence

◆ Interpretation and discussion of the findings

Your primary task in a research project is to satisfy the demands of the reader who will expect you to examine a problem, cite some of the literature about it, and offer your ideas and interpretation of it.

Exercise 3.4 Select one of the organizational models found in section 3b and develop it with your specific information. Have a friend or your instructor examine your paradigm. What questions do they raise concerning the project?

Exercise 3.5 Draft an outline for your project. List your general thesis. Below the thesis, establish several divisions that will require careful and full development. When creating the outline, consider the following questions:

What arguments will I make?

Do I need to list causes and effects?

What types of evidence can support my topic?

Title:

I. Introduction

   A. Background

     1.

     2.

   B. The problem

     1.

     2.

   C. Thesis sentence

II. The Body

   A. Major issue one

     1.

     2.

   B. Major issue two

     1.

     2.

   C. Major issue three

     1.

     2.

III. The Conclusion

   A. Review of the major issues

     1.

     2.

   B. The answer, the solution, the final opinion

     1.

     2.

CHAPTER 4

Taking Notes

A well-written research paper is built on carefully written notes. By using primary and secondary sources, you can take notes by using direct quotations, rewording ideas into a paraphrase, or giving a summary.

The primary reason for completing a research project is the sharing of information on a complex subject. You will need to support your position by citing the experts in the field, so accuracy in your quotations and paraphrases is essential.

It is essential that you write notes of high quality so that they fit appropriately into your outline, as discussed in Chapter 3. In addition, you will need to write different types of notes that reflect your evaluation of the sources. These include quotations for well-phrased passages by authorities, paraphrased notes that show your style and interpretation of the sources, and summarized notes for less-notable materials.

Consider the following strategies for taking notes. Each is explained fully in this chapter:

♦ Write a *personal note* (4b) for each of your own ideas so that you will have a set of individual concepts, not merely borrowed viewpoints or a string of borrowed quotations.

♦ Write a *direct quotation note* (4c) to share with your reader the wisdom and distinguished language of an authority.

- Write a *summary note* (4d) when you wish to explain in your own words the ideas of a particular scholar. You will interpret and restate in your words what the authority has said.

- Write a *paraphrased note* (4e) to make a quick overview of factual data that has marginal value; you can return to the source later if necessary.

4a   Creating Effective Notes

Whether you write your notes with word processing or by hand, you should keep in mind some basic rules:

Tips for creating effective notes

Write one item per note. One item of information for each note facilitates shuffling and rearranging the data as you organize your paper during all stages of organization. Several notes can be kept in a computer file if each is labeled clearly.

List the source. Abbreviate the exact source, such as "Goodspeed, 117" or Clancy, 2001, p. 32, to serve as a quick reference to the full address. Make it a practice to list the name, year, and page number on your notes. Then, you will be ready to make in-text citations for MLA, APA, or other academic styles.

Label each note. To help you arrange your notes, give it a description, such as *educational television,* or use one of your outline headings on it: *Television as a source for learning.*

Write a full note. When you have a source in your hands, write full, well-developed sentences to speed the writing of your first draft. They may later require editing to fit the context of your draft.

Keep everything. Try to save every card, sheet, scrap of paper, and note in order to authenticate a date, age, page number, or full name.

Label your personal notes. To distinguish your thoughts from those of authorities, label personal ideas with *personal note* or *my idea.*

Conform to conventions of research style. This suggestion is somewhat premature, but if you know it, write your notes to conform to your discipline—MLA or APA—as shown briefly below and explained later in this book.

Academic form of in-text citations

MLA: Karen Underwood states, "The increased number of incidents of in-air rage from passengers has many flight attendants considering other careers" (34).

APA: Underwood (2001) has commented, "The increased number of incidents of in-air rage from passengers has many flight attendants considering other careers" (p. 34).

The *default* style shown in this chapter is MLA.

Using a computer for note taking

The personal computer has made note taking an efficient part of the research process. Following are two effective methods for entering source information into a computer file:

Write each note with a separate file name in a common directory so that each can be moved later into the appropriate section of your draft by the insert commands. Build a set of files, each with its distinctive title. Periodically, you should print a copy of these notes, which should begin with the name of the file. You can then edit them on the printed sheets as well as on the computer monitor. Your instructor may also request a copy of these notes.

Write all notes in a single file, labeled with a short title, such as NOTES. It is advisable to begin each new note with a code word or phrase. When you begin the actual writing of the paper, you can begin writing at the top of the file, which will push the notes down as you write. Search out and bring up specific notes as you need them with COPY and PASTE. It is always advisable to keep a copy of the original file(s) in case anything gets lost or is deleted while arranging materials.

Remember to record the bibliographic information for each source. You can also create a bibliography file entitled "BIBLIO." The BIBLIO file will build a list of references in one alphabetical file.

Developing hand-written notes

Handwritten notes should conform to these additional conventions:

Use ink. Write notes legibly in ink because penciled notes become blurred after repeated shuffling of papers or note cards.

If you are writing by hand, *use two sizes* or *two colors of index cards,* one for notes and one for bibliography entries. This practice keeps the two separate.

Write on one side of the paper or note card.
Material on the back of a sheet or note card
may be overlooked. Staple all resources used
for one note.

4b   Writing Personal Notes

The content of a research project is not a collection
of ideas transmitted by experts in books and
articles. It is an expression of your own ideas as
supported by the scholarly evidence. Readers are
primarily interested in *your* thesis statement, *your*
topic sentences, and *your* fresh view of the issues.

As you begin researching various sources, record
your personal thoughts on the issues by writing
plenty of personal notes. Personal notes and your
writing in a research journal allow you to express
your discoveries, to reflect on the findings, to make
connections, to explore your point of view, and to
identify prevailing views and patterns of thought.

Standards for personal notes

◆ The idea on the note is exclusively yours.

◆ The note is labeled with *my idea* or *personal note*
so that later you can be certain that it has not
been borrowed.

◆ The note can be a rough summary, an abstract
sketch of ideas, or a complete sentence or two.
Most personal notes will need to be revised later
when you draft the paper.

◆ The note may list other authorities who address
this same issue.

◆ The jottings in your research journal are original and not copied from the sources.

A sample of a personal note follows:

Preventing Child Abuse   My note

Are the parents victims? The more I read, the more it seems that parents are depressed, not deranged. What causes it? I think maybe a mother who reaches a breaking point just takes it out on the kids. She doesn't hate them; she's just striking out because things are coming down hard on her.

Develop plenty of notes that record your own thoughts, or you might begin writing the paper without any original ideas.

Exercise 4.1 Take a few minutes to write at least one personal note for your research topic. Be sure to label the note as *my idea* or *personal note*. Write the note into a computer file, on notebook pages, on a note card, or in a research journal.

4c   Writing Direct Quotation Notes

The easiest type of note is one that copies the words of another person. However, you must be careful to obey a few rules.

1. You cannot copy the words of a source into

your paper in such a way that readers will think *you* wrote the material.

2. You must use the exact same words as in the source.

3. You must provide an in-text citation to the author and page number, such as (Warren 34–35).

4. You may and often should give the author's name at the beginning of the quotation and use the in-text citation at the end for page number only:

   Smithson and Myers assert, "John F. Kennedy was a victim of a centralized political plot" (42).

5. You must begin every quotation with a quotation mark and end it with a quotation mark, as shown immediately above.

6. The in-text citation goes *outside* the quotation mark but *inside* the final period.

7. The quoted material should be important and well-phrased, not something trivial or something that is common knowledge.

Correct:	"John F. Kennedy's Peace Corp left a legacy of lasting compassion for the downtrodden" (Rupert 233).
Trivial:	"John F. Kennedy was a democrat from Massachusetts" (Rupert 233).

Show the evidence of your research by using the names and page numbers of sources. Let readers, especially your teacher, see the results of your notes from books and articles.

Exercise 4.2 Five quotation notes are shown below that are based on this original material from *The World Book Encyclopedia*, Book D, page 154:

Dickens, Charles (1812–1870), was a great English novelist and one of the most popular writers of all time. His best-known books include A Christmas Carol, David Copperfield, Great Expectations, Oliver Twist, The Pickwick Papers, and A Tale of Two Cities. Dickens created some of the most famous characters in English literature. He also created scenes and descriptions of places that have delighted readers for more than a hundred years. Dickens was a keen observer of life, and had a great understanding of people. He showed sympathy for the poor and helpless, and mocked and criticized the selfish, the greedy, and the cruel.— Richard D. Altick, *World Book Encyclopedia*.

Evaluate the merits of notes A–E, using the seven criteria in (4c). Then, decide whether each of them:

1. uses exact words.

2. cites the author and the page.

3. uses quotation marks.

4. places the page citation outside the quotation mark but inside the period.

5. features material that is well-phrased and worthy of quotation.

Any *no* answer means that the particular note is unacceptable.

A. According to Richard Altick, "Dickens was a keen observer of life, and he had a great understanding of people. He showed sympathy for the poor and helpless and mocked and criticized the selfish, the greedy, and the cruel" (D-154).

B. Charles Dickens was "a wonderfully inventive comic artist. The warmth and humor of his personality appear in all his works."

C. According to Richard Altick, Charles Dickens "was a great English novelist" (D-154).

D. Charles Dickens was a keen observer of life, and had a great understanding of people. He showed sympathy for the poor and helpless and mocked and criticized the selfish, the greedy, and the cruel (Altick D-154).

E. In books such as *A Christmas Carol, Oliver Twist,* and *A Tale of Two Cities,* Charles Dickens "was a keen observer of life and had a great understanding of people" (Altick D-154).

4d   Writing Summary Notes

A summary captures the key idea of a paragraph in a few words, outlines an entire article, or provides a summary of a complete book. It has specific uses.

Plot summary. As a service to your reader, you might include a very brief summary of a novel or story:

> *Great Expectations* by Dickens describes young Pip, who inherits money and can live the life of a gentleman. But he discovers that his "great expectations" have come from a criminal. With that knowledge his attitude changes from one of vanity to one of compassion.

Review. A quick review of an article serves two purposes. In one case, you merely scan a piece of writing to jot down a few essentials in case you want to come back and read it carefully:

> Altick's article describes the life of Dickens, his books, and his place in literature.

In another type of review, you may need to write a quick note to explain something special about the work.

> The biography *Andrew Jackson* by James C. Curtis describes a president who was always full of mistrust. Curtis subtitles the book *The Search for Vindication*, which means that Jackson lived his life trying to justify his public acts and to defend his personal life.

A summary needs no citation to a page number because a summary reviews the entire work, not a specific passage.

Abstract. An abstract is a brief description of one's own paper. It is often required for a paper written in APA style (see Chapter 12). It appears at the beginning of the paper, and it helps readers decide to read or to skip an article. You will see entire books devoted to abstracts, such as *Psychological Abstracts* or *Abstracts of English Studies*.

> This study examines the problems of bullying among high school students, especially because attention most often is given only after abuse occurs, not before. With incidents of bullying on the rise, efforts devoted to prevention rather than coping should focus on the tormentors in order to discover those adolescents most likely to commit abuse because of heredity, their own childhood, the economy, and other causes of depression. Viewing the bully as a victim, not just a criminal, will enable social agencies to institute preventive programs that may control future incidents of abuse.

Exercise 4.3 Shown below are four summary notes. Select the label that best describes the nature of the summary—*plot summary, review,* or *abstract.*

1. Erikson devotes several chapters of his book *Toys and Reasons* to the play rituals in one's life cycle, from the toy age of preschoolers all the way up to adults and their toys.

2. This article will explain that children do watch television, so teachers should respond to the electronic revolution. The authors argue that television is another tool for education, but it will be an effective tool only if teachers develop a television consciousness and use the media as a supplement to other classroom methods.

3. *Le Morte d'Arthur* is Thomas Malory's early version of King Arthur, of his relations with Queen Guinevere, and of the actions of the knights of the round table, especially Lancelot, Gawain, and Galahad. Although they love their king, both Guinevere and Lancelot are unfaithful. Many knights abandon the kingdom in search of the Holy Grail. Ultimately, the death [morte] of Arthur occurs after his own son Mordred betrays him.

4. The biography *Oprah Winfrey: Media Success Story* by Anne Saidman views the life of Winfrey, from her childhood days on a farm in Mississippi to her role as talk show host.

4e   Writing Paraphrased Notes

This note is the most difficult to write. It requires you to restate in your own words the thought, meaning, and attitude of someone else. Your task is to interpret and rewrite a source in about the same number of words as the original. Keep in mind these rules for paraphrasing:

1. Retain the meaning of the original material in your restatement.

2. Like a direct quotation, a paraphrase requires an in-text citation to author and page number, like this (Millen 93). When teachers see an in-text citation but no quotation marks, they will assume that you are paraphrasing, not quoting.

3. Rewrite the material in about the same number of words.

4. Put quotation marks around any key-word phrase that you retain from the original. If you leave out any words, use ellipses, or ..., to show that words have been out.

5. You may and often should credit the source at the beginning of the paraphrase and put the page number at the end. In that way, your reader will know when the paraphrase begins and when it ends.

You can use paraphrasing to maintain the sound of your voice and style as well as to avoid an endless string of direct quotations. Here are a few examples that show how one writer paraphrased material:

> **Original:** Except for identical twins, each person's heredity is unique. —Fred V. Hein, page 294.
>
> **Paraphrase:** Fred Hein explains that heredity is

special and distinct for each of us, unless you are one of identical twins (294).

Original: Since only half of each parent's chromosomes are transmitted to a child and since this half represents a chance selection of those the child could inherit, only twins that develop from a single fertilized egg that splits in two have identical chromosomes. —Fred Hein, page 294

Paraphrase: Twins have identical chromosomes because they grow from one egg that divides after it has been fertilized (Hein 294). Most brothers and sisters differ because of the "chance selection" of chromosomes transmitted by each parent (294).

Original: Adults through the ages have been inclined to judge play to be neither serious nor useful, and thus unrelated to the center of human tasks and motives, from which the adult, in fact, seeks "recreation" when he plays. —Erikson, page 18.

Paraphrase: Adults don't think playing has much value, and Erikson says they keep it separated from their work. When adults do play, they call it "recreation" (18).

Exercise 4.4 Three paraphrased notes are shown below that are based on an original passage from a book that explains the difference between *play* and *games.*

Original: The essence of *play* is that it has no rules. . . . The essential feature of a *game* is that it involves a formal confrontation between the player and his opponent (or one player in two opposing roles) in which all activity takes place within an agreed system of rules. —John and Elizabeth Newson, p. 18.

Evaluate passages A–C below. Decide whether each of them:

1. retains the meaning of the original material.

2. uses new wording.

3. cites the original author and page.

4. uses quotation marks for any original phrasing.

A. It seems to me that children left alone have lots of fun. When a so-called game begins, we need referees and coaches and rule books. According to one source, the difference between merely playing and playing a game is the rules. The rules seem to establish a "formal confrontation" (Newson 18).

B. When we make up games on the playground, we are playing and having fun, but when we participate in little league baseball or soccer, the rules of the game become very important, so important in fact that we need referees and rule books and screaming parents to resolve the formal confrontations.

C. John and Elizabeth Newson explain the difference between playing for fun and playing a game. They say that play "has no rules," and they say that playing a game "involves a formal confrontation" (18). Maybe that's why the fun disappears when children get into a little league game dominated by referees, rules, and screaming parents.

Exercise 4.5 Below is an original statement about Ernest Hemingway's novel *The Old Man and the Sea*.

Original: The story has been interpreted as a symbolic tale of man's courage and dignity in the face of defeat.
—Philip Young, World Book Encyclopedia, H-173.

1. Write a note that *quotes* Philip Young.

2. Write a note that *paraphrases* Philip Young.

4f   Selecting a Mix of Both Primary and Secondary Sources

Primary sources are the original words of a writer, such as a novel, poem, play, short story, letter, autobiography, speech, report, film, television program, design, computer program, or interview.

Secondary sources are works about somebody (biography) or about a creative work (critical evaluation). Secondary sources are an interpretation of a novel or painting, a review of a play or movie, or a biography of a famous person's life and work. Other secondary evaluations may appear as news reports, some magazine articles that evaluate people, places, and things, or textbooks, which evaluate events, literary works, and discoveries.

Think of secondary sources as pieces of writing *about* the primary sources and *about* the creators of primary works. In general, you should paraphrase secondary sources, not quote them, unless the wording of the original is especially well-phrased. However, you should quote primary sources.

Primary Source:

> *We Real Cool*
> *The Pool Players*
> *Seven at the Golden Shovel*
>
> We real cool. We
> Left School. We
> Lurk late. We
> Strike straight. We
> Sing sin. We
> Thin gin. We
> Jazz June. We
> Die soon.
> —Gwendolyn Brooks
> from *Crossing Cultures*, page 155

Secondary Source:

> When Gwendolyn Brooks writes about conditions in the African American community, her ethnic dialect rings true and her message is filled appropriately with tragic awareness. —Lawrence Wright from *Modern Poets on the Edge*, page 8.

Student's note using the primary source:

> Gwendolyn Brooks has her seven pool players brag. They say "We real cool" and "We Sing sin." But she also shows the bad side of that kind of life, "We Die soon" (155).

Student's note using the secondary source:

> One critic says Gwendolyn Brooks knows her people. He says her "black dialect rings true" in "We Real Cool" and the poem also shows her "tragic awareness" (Wright 8).

Student's note using both the primary and the secondary sources:

> When Gwendolyn Brooks has her seven pool players at the Golden Shovel say, "We real cool," she captures the voice and the attitude of young African Americans (155). When they say, "We Die soon," Brooks shows, according to Lawrence Wright, her tragic awareness (8).

 Exercise 4.6 Decide which of the types of writing below are primary sources.

novel	book review
play	literary interpretation
biography	evaluation of a poem
speech	interview
song	a textbook's introduction to a poem
poem	letter

4g   Avoiding Plagiarism

Plagiarism is purposely using another person's writing as your own. You cannot present as your own another person's words, music, or drawings without providing a citation to that person. Plagiarism occurs when you purposely and knowingly commit one of these errors:

◆ You turn in another student's paper as your own.

◆ You copy portions of another student's paper into your own.

◆ You copy source material into your paper without quotation marks and without an in-text citation to author and page.

◆ You paraphrase source material into your paper without an in-text citation to author and page.

◆ You summarize source material without a clear reference to the original source.

Plagiarism violates the academic code of conduct. In your research paper, you must give credit to others for their words and ideas. Granted, there are exceptions for common knowledge. Most people know that George Washington was our first president and that he lived at Mount Vernon. However, if one source says Washington often ignored his Secretary of State, Thomas Jefferson, to seek the wisdom of Alexander Hamilton, his Secretary of the Treasury, then a citation to the source would be in order.

Therefore, make it a regular practice to identify your sources within your text. Label all notes and references carefully to assure yourself that full credit has been given to the sources. Always label your note with a descriptive title, the author, and the exact page numbers. Below is a quotation from a source, followed by sample notes.

Original:

> If young adult novels seem depressing, we should remember that adolescence is often a difficult time of life, and most YA novels effectively mirror those difficulties. It's interesting that this criticism comes almost always from adults rather than from young adult readers. Again, the concern may stem from our own memories of adolescence—or from our desire to remember it differently from the way we actually experienced it. In any case, it's art imitating life, and young adult readers know this better than anyone.
> —Virginia R. Monseau, "From the Editor," *English Journal* Jan. 2001: 17.

Following are three notes that demonstrate the proper citation of a source in order to avoid plagiarism.

> One authority views young adult literature as an imitation for what is really happening in the world, and, most importantly, in the lives of adolescents (Monseau 17).

> Virginia Monseau relates that many young adult novels convey sad themes, but we should remember that "adolescence is often a difficult time of life" (17).

> "This criticism comes almost always from adults," says Virginia Monseau, but we must realize that "young adult readers know better than anyone" (17).

Exercise 4.7 Evaluate Notes 1–6 below. Decide whether each is a proper citation of original information or a common knowledge fact.

Original:

> Alabama, one of the Southern states, is known as the *Heart of Dixie*. Alabama occupies a central place in the history of the South. The Constitution of the

Confederacy was drawn up in Montgomery, the state capital. The Alabama capital served as the first confederate capital. There, Jefferson Davis took office as President of the Confederacy.

Today, Alabama has a vital part in the nation's future. Huntsville, called *Rocket City, U.S.A.,* is the site of the Redstone Arsenal and the Marshall Space Flight Center. Scientists at Huntsville developed many important rockets and space vehicles, including the Mercury-Redstone rocket system that carried the U.S. astronauts into space.

Most parts of the South did not become widely industrialized until the 1900s. But heavy industry got a relatively early start in Alabama, mainly because of the state's rich mineral resources. Northern Alabama is one of the few areas in the world that has all three main raw materials used in making steel—coal, iron ore, and limestone. Blast furnaces for making iron and steel began operating in Birmingham in the 1880s. After that, Birmingham grew rapidly. Today, it is Alabama's largest city. "Alabama," *Encarta Encyclopedia,* 2000.

1. Northern Alabama is one of the few areas in the world that has all three main raw materials used in making steel—coal, iron ore, and limestone.

2. Alabama, called the "Heart of Dixie," has a strong industrial base with Birmingham as the hub.

3. One source says that "heavy industry got a relatively early start in Alabama, mainly because of the state's rich mineral resources" ("Alabama").

4. Most of the South did not become industrialized until late in the 1800s, but Alabama got an early start because of its rich mineral resources used in making steel—coal, iron ore, and limestone ("Alabama").

5. Scientists at Huntsville developed many important rockets and space vehicles, including the Mercury-Redstone rocket system that carried the U.S. astronauts into space.

6. While other southern cities failed to attract industry, Birmingham, thanks to vast mineral deposits, developed a large industrial base in the 1880s ("Alabama").

Avoiding plagiarism

1. Introduce the quotation or paraphrase with the name of the authority or place the authority's name with the page number inside the parentheses at the end of the citation.

2. Enclose all direct quotations within quotation marks.

3. Rewrite paraphrased material in your own style and language; do not simply rearrange sentence phrases.

4. At the end of each summary, paraphrase, or direct quotation, provide a specific page number within parentheses unless the material came from an Internet source, in which case you omit any page or paragraph numbers. If you have not introduced the material with the name of the author, include the name here.

5. For every source mentioned within the paper, you must provide a bibliographic entry on the "Works Cited" page.

Exercise 4.8 Evaluate Notes 1–5 below. Decide whether each is an effective use of source materials or is plagiarism. Here is the source, which includes the primary words of author Louis L'Amour and the secondary commentary of the *Current Biography* editors:

> Despite their frequent references to gunplay, intermittent gunfights, and occasional instances of cannibalism, tortures, and hanging, L'Amour's books, compared with those of his rivals, are free of gratuitous violence. L'Amour contends that guns are "over-stressed" in most westerns and likes to remind interviewers that from 1800 to 1816 "there were as many gunfights in our Navy as on the entire frontier." "My whole feeling about the American West, the American frontier, is that a lot more was happening than just a bunch of gunfights or Indian battles," he told Ned Smith. "A lot of cultures were meeting, a lot of influences came together."—from "Louis L'Amour," *1980 Current Biography*, page 205.

1. L'Amour's books make frequent references to gunplay, to intermittent gunfights, and to tortures, but he doesn't overdo it and argues that more was happening than just a bunch of gunfights or Indian battles.

2. "My whole feeling about the American West, the American frontier," says L'Amour, "is that a lot more was happening than just a bunch of gunfights or Indian battles" (*Current Biography* 205).

3. One biography argues that L'Amour's fiction, when compared with other westerns, is "free of gratuitous violence," though his writing does have its share of fighting, Indian wars, and occasional hangings (*Current Biography* 205).

4. Louis L'Amour was fascinated by the mix of people and ethnic races on the western frontier. "A lot of cultures were meeting," he said at one

point, "a lot of influences came together" (*Current Biography* 205).

5. L'Amour contends that guns are "over-stressed" in most westerns and likes to remind interviewers that from 1800 to 1816 "there were as many gunfights in our Navy as on the entire frontier."

CHAPTER 5

Writing with an Academic Style

Even though a research project aims for a more formal style than you might use in a personal essay, the writing should nevertheless read well. Your voice should flow smoothly and logically from one idea to the next, expressing clear and precise ideas.

The research project examines your knowledge and the strength of your evidence. You may need to retrace previous steps—reading, researching, and note taking. Ask your instructor to read through the draft to see if the main parts have sequence, logic, and reasonable development. Most instructors are more than willing to give your draft a summary reading.

An academic style also requires precise wording. Every discipline has its own specialized words, and researching a topic should prompt you to find the key terms in your area of research and use them effectively.

Drafting is a process of many starts and stops, so do not expect a polished product at first. Meals, classes, activities, and even daydreaming slow down the composing process. Your first draft is exploratory and will require further reading, researching, and note taking.

Three rules for drafting may serve your needs:

- **Be practical.** Begin by writing portions of the project when you are ready, not after you have a complete outline. Write what you know about the subject, not what you think somebody wants to hear.

- **Be uninhibited.** Initial drafts must be attempts to get words on the page rather than a finished document. Write without fear or delay.

- **Be judicious.** Remember that a first draft is a time for discovery. Later, during the revision period, you can strengthen your paragraphs, refine your writing style, and rearrange material to maintain the momentum of your position.

5a Focusing Your Argument

Your writing style in a research project needs to be factual, but it should also display human emotion. Develop your project around your feelings about the topic as well as the facts of the study. You will convince the audience of your point of view in two ways:

Ethical appeal. The reader will recognize your deep interest in the subject and your carefully crafted argument if you project the image of one who knows and cares about the topic.

Logical appeal. For readers to believe in your topic, you must provide sufficient evidence in the form of statistics, paraphrases, and direct quotations from authorities on the subject.

When considering the topic of *urban sprawl,* a writer might remain objective in presenting the evidence and statistics; yet, the ethical problem remains close to the surface: green spaces and natural habitats of animals are quickly disappearing. Your aim or purpose is the key to discovering an argument. Do you wish to persuade, inquire, or negotiate?

Persuasion means that you wish to convince the reader that your position is valid and, perhaps, to ask the reader to take action. For example:

> We need to establish parks, playgrounds, and green zones in every city of this country to control urban sprawl and to protect a segment of the natural habitat for the animals.

Inquiry is an exploratory approach to a problem in which you examine the issues without the insistence of persuasion. It is a truth-seeking adventure. For example:

> Many suburban homeowners complain that deer, raccoons, and other wild animals ravage their gardens, flowerbeds, and garbage cans; however, the animals were there first. For this reason, we need to consider the rights of each side in this conflict.

Negotiation is a search for a solution. It means that you attempt to resolve a conflict by inventing options or a mediated solution. For example:

> Suburban neighbors need to find ways to embrace the wild animals that have been displaced rather than voice anger at the animals or the county government. Perhaps green zones and wilderness trails would solve some of the problems. However, such a solution would require serious negotiations with real estate developers who want to use every square foot of space.

As you begin the drafting process, it is essential to read over the instructions from your teacher. Often, the instructor's research assignment will tell you whether you want to persuade, inquire, or negotiate. Underline key words in the directions to make sure you address all major parts of the assignment. If the assignment does not specify its purpose, try to determine early in the process where your research is heading.

5b Drafting the Thesis Statement

A thesis is a statement or idea supported by arguments. Make sure your thesis statement satisfies all the following requirements:

1. State your argument or idea to give focus to the entire paper.

2. Provide unity and a sense of direction.

3. Specify to the reader the point of the research.

For example, one student established a thesis that addresses children sitting in automobiles equipped with air bags:

> Automobile air bags were mandated by Congress to save lives, but the design and/or the engineering endangers children and small adults.

Using questions to focus the thesis

If you have trouble focusing on a thesis statement, ask yourself a few questions. One of the answers might serve as a thesis.

What is the point of my research?

> **Thesis:** Recent research demonstrates that self-guilt often prompts a teenager to commit suicide.

What do I want this paper to do?

>**Thesis:** The public needs to understand that water restrictions during a drought are enacted to benefit all citizens.

Can I tell the reader anything new or different?

>**Thesis:** Like the legends of lost mines, buried treasure, or ghosts, urban legends usually have an ironic or supernatural twist.

Do I have a solution to the problem?

>**Thesis:** Public support for "safe" houses will provide a haven for children who are abused by their parents.

Do I have a new slant and new approach to the issue?

>**Thesis:** Written allusions to great works of literature and the Bible no longer have special significance because those works are unfamiliar to a growing number of people.

Should I take the minority view of this matter?

>**Thesis:** Regardless of the negative view of political matters that stemmed from the corruption of his administration, Richard Nixon will go down as one of the greatest peacemakers of all time.

What exactly is my theory about this subject?

>**Thesis:** Trustworthy employees, not mechanical safeguards on computers and software, will prevent theft of software, sabotage of mainframes, and destruction of crucial files.

Using key words to focus the thesis

Use the important words from your notes and rough outline to improve your thesis statement. For example, during your reading of several short stories by Flannery O'Connor, you might have jotted down certain repetitions of image, theme, or character. The key words might be "death," "ironic moments of humor," "human shortcomings," or other issues that O'Connor explored time and again. These concrete ideas might point you toward a general thesis:

> The tragic endings of Flannery O'Connor's stories depict desperate people coming face-to-face with their own shortcomings.

Final Thesis Checklist

- ◆ It expresses your position in a full, declarative sentence, which is not a question, not a statement of purpose, and not merely a topic.

- ◆ It limits the subject to a narrow focus on one issue that has grown out of research.

- ◆ It establishes an investigative, inventive edge to your research and gives a reason for all your work.

- ◆ It points forward to the conclusion.

- ◆ It prompts you to seek evidence in the library.

Exercise 5.1 Using the Final Thesis Checklist as your guide, evaluate the following ten thesis statements as *good, adequate,* or *poor.* If you decide that any of the statements are poor, show on a separate sheet of notebook paper how you might revise and correct them.

1. The purpose of this paper is to tell you about water quality and how pollution affects it.

2. The poetry of Robert Frost exhibits a fascination with images of darkness.

3. It is ironic that we live in a society that

condemns violence yet supports a variety of violent sporting events.

4. Rap music is always vibrant and lively.

5. For many children, school is a place of trouble, and their main business of the day is staying out of trouble as much as possible.

6. In the United States, a woman's place is no longer in the home.

7. The initiation story is a type of narrative.

8. Ernest Hemingway's *The Old Man and the Sea* is about an old man, a fish, and a boy.

9. Tae Kwon Do can provide relief from psychological fatigue.

10. Country music is filled with heartache and sorrow.

5c Writing a Title for Your Project

Like a good thesis statement, a clearly expressed title, developed early in the composing process, will control your writing and keep you on course. However, a title may not be feasible until the paper is written. Your task is to give the reader a clear concept about the contents of your project, so use one of these strategies for writing your title:

1. Name a general subject, followed by a colon and a phrase that focuses or shows your slant on the subject.

   Bill Gates: Computer Industry Giant

2. Narrow a general subject with a prepositional phrase.

>   Poverty in the Suburbs

3. Name a general subject and cite a specific work that will clarify the topic.

>   Christian Symbols in Herman Melville's *Billy Budd*

4. Name a general subject, followed by a colon, and followed by a phrase that describes the type of study.

>   Black Dialect in *Huckleberry Finn*: A Language Study

5. Name a general subject, followed by a colon, and followed by a question.

>   Electric Cars: What are Automakers Waiting For?

Be sure to avoid fancy literary titles that may fail to label issues under discussion.

Poor: An American Folk Hero

Better: Folk Heros of the Wild West

Best: Buffalo Bill: An American Folk Hero

For placement of the title, see Section 11a, "Formatting the Paper," pages 144–147.

Exercise 5.2 Evaluate whether each of the following research project titles is *acceptable* or *unacceptable*. If you think that a title is unacceptable, revise it by rewriting it on a separate sheet of paper.

1. Fishing at Lake Jodeco

2. Signals of Pleasure: Affordable Satellite Television

3. The Ozark Region of Arkansas

4. How to Win Lottery Money

5. Raising Buffalo in Nebraska: New Range Policies

6. Realities of War in "An Occurrence at Owl Creek Bridge"

7. Social Issues in the Music of Garth Brooks

8. The Short Stories of James Thurber

9. Religions in America

10. Social Protest in the 1500s: Pirates in the Western Hemisphere

5d Drafting from Your Notes and Outline

As you begin drafting your research paper, you may work steadily through the outline to keep order as your notes expand the outline. Your notes let the essay reach new levels of knowledge. You may also start anywhere in the outline in order to write what you know at the time, keeping the pieces of manuscript controlled by your thesis and overall plan.

In the rough draft, feel free to leave wide margins, use triple spacing, and have blank spaces between some paragraphs. Open areas in your initial writing will help you make revisions and add parts later on. The process is simplified with a personal computer because the information is keyboarded one time and revisions can take place at the computer screen. Use your notes and research journal to:

◆ Transfer and modify personal notes into the draft.

- Write paraphrased materials directly into the text.

- Quote primary sources.

- Quote secondary sources from notes.

Write with caution when working from photocopied pages of articles or books. You will be tempted to borrow too much. Quote or paraphrase key phrases and sentences. Do not quote an entire paragraph unless it is crucial to your discussion and you cannot easily reduce it to a summary.

When drafting on a computer, it is crucial that you save your work often to avoid the aggravation of losing information. To avoid the loss of your text, create new files on your computer for each new version of the report.

Incorporating source material into paragraphs

Readers want to discover your thoughts and ideas. For this reason, a paragraph should seldom contain source material only; it needs at least a topic sentence to establish your view of the research evidence. Every paragraph should explain, analyze, and support a thesis, not merely string together research information. The following passage effectively cites two different sources.

> Faced with hot, dry summers, many gardeners in the southeastern United States have discovered the value of drought resistant plants. Two factors that play a part in some lands becoming drought-prone are "light, sandy soil and soils with high alkalinity" (Allen and Graber 122). The best drought resistant plants come from countries that border the Mediterranean Sea (Bjornson 26).

This passage illustrates four points. A writer must:

- Weave the sources effectively into a whole.

- Cite each source separately, one at a time.

- Provide different in-text citations.

- Use the sources as a natural extension of the discussion.

A complete discussion for incorporating sources into your paper is found in Chapter 6, "Combining Sources in Your Writing."

It is important to document information that is borrowed from sources. However, at times, you will not need to provide a citation for general information, also called **common knowledge exceptions.** Common knowledge exceptions include ideas that are known by a majority of persons or ideas that are from your own personal reflection on the topic.

Checklist for Common Knowledge Exceptions

- Would an intelligent person know this information?

- Did you know the information before you discovered it in a source?

- Is it encyclopedia-type information?

- Has this information become general knowledge by being reported repeatedly and in many different sources?

Exercise 5.3 Evaluate each of the following items below. Decide whether each of them should be documented. Refer to Section 4g for notes on plagiarism.

1. The fact that historian Atchley McCormick mentions that John Adams was the first

president to occupy the White House.

2. A paraphrase of a source.

3. A note from historian Mitchell Michaels that Franklin Pierce secretly tried to block the Compromise of 1850.

4. Your personal notes, including your thesis statement.

5. The source of the phrase: "red blood cells transfer oxygen to the tissues."

Writing in the proper tense

Verb tense often distinguishes a paper in the humanities from one in the natural and social sciences. Developed by the Modern Language Association, MLA style requires the present tense to cite an author's work, such as, *Stevens explains* or *the work of Allard and Whitaker shows*. The example below demonstrates the correct verb tense in MLA style:

> The availability and convenience of credit cards has been both a blessing and a curse for today's consumers. Kaitlin Young argues that the credit card has become "an agent of debt, of spending addiction, and of a loss of privacy" (67).

For a complete and detailed explanation on writing this kind of passage, refer to Chapter 6, "Combining Sources in Your Writing."

In contrast, APA style, under the direction of the American Psychological Association, requires the past tense or present perfect tense to cite an author's work, as in *Stevens discovered* or *the work of Allard and Whitaker has demonstrated*. APA style is primarily used in social studies courses. The example below shows the correct verb tense in APA style:

> Givens and Peterson (2001) argued that, too often, credit cards are issued to applicants who have no bank account, a poor credit history, and no job (2001, p. 23).

A complete and detailed explanation for using APA style is given in Chapter 12, "Handling Format — APA Style."

Use the past tense in a humanities paper only for reporting historical events. In the next example, past tense is appropriate for all sentences except the last:

> In 1876, Alexander Graham Bell invented the telephone. Signals, sounds, and music had been sent by wire before, but Bell's instrument was the first to transmit speech. Bell's story, a lesson in courage and determination, is one worthy of study.

Writing in the third person

Write your paper with narration that avoids phrases such as *I believe* or *It is my opinion*. Following is an example of incorrect writing, and a revision that corrects the error. Even in the correction, the readers will understand that the statement is your thought.

Incorrect: I think that setting term limits for politicians would eliminate legislators who become professional politicians.

Correct: Setting term limits for politicians would eliminate legislators who become professional politicians.

Using the language of the discipline

Every discipline and every topic has its own

vocabulary. Therefore, while reading and taking notes, jot down words and phrases that are related to the study. Get comfortable with the vocabulary of your topic so you can use it effectively. For example, a child abuse topic requires the language of sociology, psychology, and medicine, thereby demanding technical terms like:

aggressive behavior	maltreatment
battered child	social worker
behavioral patterns	stress
formative years	trauma
hostility	

Example:

> The hostility that builds silently in a battered child can result in aggressive behavior in the emerging teenager.

Writing with unity and coherence

Unity gives writing a single vision, and **coherence** connects the parts. Your paper has unity if it explores one topic in depth, with each paragraph carefully expanding upon a single aspect of the narrowed subject. A good organizational plan will help you achieve unity. Your paper has coherence if the parts are connected logically by:

◆ repetition of key words and sentence structures,

◆ the judicious use of pronouns and synonyms, and

◆ the effective placement of transitional words and phrases (e.g., *also, furthermore, therefore, in addition*, and *thus*).

The next passage moves with unity and coherence:

> Talk shows are spectacles of dramatic entertainment; therefore, members of the studio audience are acting out parts in the drama, like a Greek chorus, just as the host, the guest, and the television viewers are actors as well. Furthermore, some sort of interaction with the "characters" in this made-for-television "drama" happens all the time. If we read a book or attend a play, we question the text, we question the presentation, and we determine for ourselves what it means to us.

Using graphics in a research project

Graphics enable you to analyze trends and relationships in numerical data. When appropriate, use them to support your text. Most computers allow you to create tables, line graphs, or pie charts as well as diagrams, maps, and other original designs. You may also import tables and illustrations from your sources.

Graphics must be placed as close as possible to the parts of the text to which they relate. It is acceptable to use full-color art if your printer will print in colors, but you should use black for the captions and date. Place a full-page graphic design on a separate sheet after making a textual reference to it, such as, *See Table 4*. Place graphic designs in an appendix when you have several complex items that might distract the reader from your textual message.

CHAPTER 6

Combining Sources in Your Writing

You will be using references to other sources throughout your paper. Established by the Modern Language Association, MLA style requires you to list an author and a page number in your text, usually within parentheses. Notice how this next passage uses names and page numbers.

> The *cell theory* was developed in the late 19th century. "Scientists discovered single cells that divided into two identical offspring cells" (Hartley 56). Irene Justice explains the two parts of the cell theory: "All organisms are composed of cells and all cells derive from other living cells" (131).

Another style is the American Psychological Association name-and-year system (see pages 158–172).

6a Using References in Your Text

As a general policy, provide just enough information within the text to identify a source. Readers will have full documentation to each source on the Works Cited page.

Begin with the author and end with a page number.

Introduce a quotation or a paraphrase with the author's name and close with a page number, placed inside parentheses:

> Herbert Norfleet states that the use of video games by children improves their hand and eye coordination (45).

This paraphrase makes absolutely clear to the reader when the borrowed idea begins and when it ends.

Notice how unclear the use of the source can become when the writer does not introduce borrowed material:

> The use of video games by children improves their hand and eye coordination. Children also exercise their minds by working their way through various puzzles and barriers. "The mental gymnastics of video games and the competition with fellow players are important to young children and their development physically, socially, and mentally" (Norfleet 45).

What was borrowed? It seems that only the final quotation came from Norfleet. Yet in truth, the entire paragraph, the paraphrasing and the quotation, came from Norfleet. Norfleet is the expert for this paragraph, so the paper should mention his name prominently, as shown below:

> Herbert Norfleet defends the use of video games by children. He says it improves their hand and eye coordination and that it exercises their minds as they work their way through various puzzles and barriers. Norfleet states, "The mental gymnastics of video games and the competition with fellow players are important to young children and their development physically, socially, and mentally" (45).

This paragraph conforms to MLA style because it:

◆ credits the source properly and honestly.

♦ shows the correct use of both paraphrase and quotation.

♦ demonstrates the student's research into the subject.

Remember that an important reason for writing a research paper is to gather and present source material on a topic, so it only follows that you should display those sources prominently in your writing, not hide them or fail to cite them.

Exercise 6.1 The following passage has a citation to name and page at the end of the last sentence, but in truth the entire paraphrased passage has been borrowed. Edit it to give credit throughout the paragraph to the original source, Charles R. Larson, *American Indian Fiction*, page 17.

There is one story that lies deep in our reaction to American Indians—Pocahontas. It is "a living myth that will not die." But the distortions of the Pocahontas story cause us to misread and misunderstand subsequent writings by Indian writers (Larson 17).

Put the name and page number at the end of borrowed material.

You can, if you like, put the authority's name and the page number at the end of a quotation or paraphrase, but give your reader a signal to show when the borrowing begins.

> One source explains that the DNA in the chromosomes must be copied perfectly during cell reproduction. "Each DNA strand provides the pattern of bases for a new strand to form, resulting in two complete molecules" (Justice, Moody, and Graves 462).

Exercise 6.2 The following passage cites the authority's name and page only at the end of the passage. The first two sentences are common knowledge, but the final three sentences of the passage were borrowed directly from Robert Barnett. Edit the passage to show when the borrowing begins.

After she learned the concept of language from Anne Sullivan, Helen Keller began to develop her amazing intellect. She learned to speak and earned a degree at Radcliffe College in 1904. Unlocked from her own handicaps, she began her devoted efforts to help the blind and other handicapped persons. She made frequent lectures to raise money for the American Foundation for the Blind. Later, she donated two million dollars to establish the Helen Keller Endowment Fund (Barnett 210).

Establishing the credibility of the source

An excellent approach for blending a source into the text of your research paper is to indicate the source's scholarly value. For example, the following example introduces the author and the organization for which she is working:

> Jennifer Sahn, Assistant Director of the Orion Society, promotes educational programs that can "heal the fractured relationship between people and nature." Moreover, she supports changes in "ethics and action at the local level that will offer genuine solutions to the global environmental crisis."

It is crucial that you check the validity of an Internet source (see pages 32–33). To learn more about the source of an Internet article, as in the case immediately above, learn to search its **home page.** The address for Sahn's article is:

<http://www.orionsociety.org/mission.html>

6b   Citing a Source When No Author Is Listed

When no author is shown on a title page, cite the title of an article, the name of the magazine, the name of a bulletin or book, or the name of the publishing organization. Look for the author's name at the bottom of the opening page and at the end of the article.

Citing a title of a report and a page number

> One bank showed a significant decline in assets despite an increase in its number of depositors (*Annual Report* 23).

Citing a title of a magazine article and a page number

> "In one sense toys serve as a child's tools, and by learning to use the toys the child stimulates physical and mental development" ("Selling" 37).

Note: You should shorten magazine titles to a key word for the citation. You must then give the full title in the works cited entry (see Chapter 10).

Citing a publisher or corporate body and a page number

> The report by the school board endorsed the use of Channel One in the school system and said that "students will benefit by the news reports more than they will be adversely affected by advertising" (Clarion County School Board 3–4).

Exercise 6.3 Write the in-text citation for this next passage as if the information came from page 344 of an unpublished report by Dayton Holding Company.

One financial institution suggests that each high school

graduate should receive a $10,000 grant that could be used for college, for starting a business, for savings, or to begin a marriage on a sound financial basis (   ).

6c   Citing Non-print Sources

On occasion, you may need to identify non-print sources, such as a speech, the song lyrics from a compact disk, an interview, or something you have heard on television. In these cases, there will be no page number, so you can omit the parenthetical citation. Instead, introduce the nature of the source so that your reader will not expect a page number.

Citing a source that has no page number

Thompson's lecture defined *impulse* as "an action triggered by the nerves without thought for the consequences."

Mrs. Peggy Meacham said in her phone interview that prejudice against young African American women is not as severe as that against young African American males.

In his rap song, Julian Young cries out to young people with this message, "Stay in the school, man, stay in the school; learn how to rule, man, learn how to rule."

Exercise 6.4 Write a passage with the correct in-text citation to a television program on CBS-TV during which an announcer said, "The President's policy toward homeless people appears nonexistent."

6d   Citing Internet Sources

Most Internet sources have no designated page numbers or numbered paragraphs. You cannot list the screen numbers or the page numbers of a downloaded document because computer screens and printers differ. Therefore, provide a paragraph or a page number *only* if the author of the Internet article has provided it.

The marvelous feature of electronic text is that it is searchable, so your readers can find your quotation quickly with the URL and the browser's **FIND** feature. The following paragraph features information from an Internet source:

> One Internet source polled adolescents and found that 54 percent of all teens believed their schools were becoming too violent, 15 percent feared being shot or hurt by a classmate carrying weapons to school, and 22 percent were afraid to go into school restrooms because these unsupervised areas were frequent sites where violence took place (Society for School Violence Prevention 3).

A reader who wants to investigate further will find your complete citation on your Works Cited page. There, the reader will discover the URL address of the article.

6e   Citing Indirect Sources

Sometimes the writer of a magazine or newspaper article will quote another person, and you want to use that same quotation. For example, in a newspaper article in *USA Today,* page 9A, Karen S. Peterson writes this passage in which she quotes another person:

Sexuality, popularity, and athletic competition will create anxiety for junior high kids and high schoolers, Eileen Shiff says. "Bring up the topics. Don't wait for them to do it; they are nervous and they want to appear cool. Monitor the amount of time high schoolers spend working for money," she suggests. "Work is important, but school must be the priority."

Parental intervention in a child's school career that worked in junior high may not work in high school, psychiatrist Martin Greenburg adds. "The interventions can be construed by the adolescent as negative, overburdening, and interfering with the child's ability to care for himself." He adds, "Be encouraging, not critical. Criticism can be devastating for the teenager."

Suppose that you want to use the quotation by Martin Greenburg. You will need to cite both Greenburg, the speaker, and Peterson who wrote the article. Notice that *qtd.* is the abbreviation for *quoted.*

After students get beyond middle school, they begin to resent interference by their parents, especially in school-related activities. Martin Greenburg says, "The interventions can be construed by the adolescent as negative, overburdening, and interfering with the child's ability to care for himself" (qtd. In Peterson 9A).

As shown above, you need a double reference that introduces the speaker but that also includes a clear reference to the book or article where you found the quotation or the paraphrased material. Without the reference to Peterson, nobody could find the article. Without the reference to Greenburg, readers would assume that Peterson wrote the words. Peterson's name will appear on a bibliographic entry on your Works Cited page, but Greenburg's will not because Greenburg is not the author of the article.

Exercise 6.5 An author named Shirley Nash wrote an article on sports medicine in which she quoted a man named Peter Evans on page 91 and a man named Hollis Landover on page 68. Complete the in-text citations.

Peter Evans condemns any advertising that "encourages people to overeat and overdrink" (   ).

Even musicians are subject to sports injuries. Hollis Landover says, "Extended practice sessions as well as the gyrations on stage can cause serious injury to musical performers" (   ).

6f Citing Material from Textbooks and Anthologies

If you quote a passage from a textbook or anthology, and if that is all that you quote from the source, cite the author and page in the text and put a complete entry on the Works Cited page. In the text, write:

> In "The Fish" Elizabeth Bishop compares "five old pieces of fish-line" caught in the lip of the ancient fish to "medals with their ribbons frayed and wavering" (542).

For the bibliography entry on the Works Cited page, write:

> Bishop, Elizabeth. "The Fish." *The Compact Bedford Introduction to Literature.* Ed. Michael Meyer. Boston: Bedford/St. Martins, 2000. 542.

6g Adding Information to In-Text Citations

As a courtesy to your reader, add extra information within a citation. Show parts of books, different titles by the same writer, or several works by different writers. For example, your reader may have a different anthology than yours, so a reference to *Great Expectations*, Ch. 4, 681, will enable the reader to locate the passage. The same is true with a reference to *Romeo and Juliet* 2.3.65–68. The reader will find the passage in any edition of the Shakespearean play by turning to Act 2, Scene 3, lines 65–68.

Citing one of several volumes

> In a letter to his Tennessee Volunteers in 1812, General Jackson chastised the "mutinous and disorderly conduct" of some of his troops (*Papers* 2: 348–49).

The citation above gives an abbreviation for the title (*The Papers of Andrew Jackson*), the volume used, and the page numbers.

Citing two or more works of the same writer

> Thomas Hardy reminds readers in his prefaces that "a novel is an impression, not an argument" and that a novel should be read as "a study of man's deeds and character"(*Tess* xxii; *Mayor* 1).

The writer above makes reference to two different novels, both abbreviated. Full titles are *Tess of the D'Urbervilles* and *The Mayor of Casterbridge*. Remember that it is acceptable to abbreviate in parenthetical citations, but not in your text.

Citing several authors who have written on the same topic

> Several sources have addressed this aspect of gang warfare as a fight for survival, not just for turf (Rollins 34; Templass 561–65; Robertson 98–134).

The citation above refers to three different writers who address the same topic.

Exercise 6.6 Evaluate the following sentences. Decide whether their use of references is *correct* or *incorrect.* Keep in mind the lesson on plagiarism (4g).

Original source:

> We hold these truths to be self-evident, that all men are created equal, that they are endowed by their Creator with certain unalienable Rights, that among these are Life, Liberty and the pursuit of Happiness.
> —Thomas Jefferson, "Declaration of Independence," paragraph 1.

1. In the "Declaration of Independence," Thomas Jefferson says that "all men are created equal" and that every person has a right to "Life, Liberty and the pursuit of Happiness" (para. 1).

2. If you accept the point of view that truth is often self-evident, then you must agree that all of us are created equal and therefore have equal rights.

3. One patriot defended the "unalienable rights" of Americans to "Life, Liberty and the pursuit of Happiness" (Jefferson para. 1).

Original source:

> O. Henry's criminal conviction and prison term was for some time the most uncertain and controversial aspect of his life. One of his biographers, Al Jennings, who was in the penitentiary with O. Henry, recounts that the

writer's greatest fear was that he would be recognized and greeted by a former inmate while in the company of others. Many of O. Henry's closest acquaintances never knew that he had spent time in prison, and he often juggled dates to account for the years spent in prison. — "O. Henry," *Twentieth Century Literary Criticism*, page 166.

4. Many people did not know that O. Henry, the famous short story writer, spent time in prison. He carefully juggled dates to account for the years spent in prison.

5. According to Al Jennings, who spent time in prison with the writer, O. Henry feared that a former inmate might identify him in the presence of friends or relatives (cited in "O. Henry" 166).

6. Al Jennings said that O. Henry juggled dates to account for the years spent in prison (cited in "O. Henry" 166).

7. A known fact is that O. Henry was a great writer of short stories.

Original source:

Communications satellites can be sized and configured in a variety of ways, involving different capacities and power levels, alternate means of onboard propulsion and stabilization, varying useful lifetimes (including the possibility of manned or unmanned maintenance), adaptation to different boosters, and, for military satellites, incorporation of various survivability measures against hostile environments.
— George Gerbner, "Communications Satellite," *The Encyclopedia Americana*, page 431.

8. Communication satellites can be sized and configured in a variety of ways, involving different capacities and power levels.

9. One article explains that communications

satellites have various sizes and lifetimes, and engineers can change propulsion, use different boosters, and incorporate military armaments (Gerbner 431).

10. Communications satellites have various sizes and lifetimes, and engineers can change propulsion, use different boosters, and incorporate military armaments (from the *Encyclopedia America,* page 431).

6h   Indenting Long Quotations

Set off long quotations of four or more lines by indenting ten (10) spaces. Do not use quotation marks around the indented material. Place the parenthetical citation *after* the final period of the quotation, not inside the period.

> In his book *A Time to Heal,* Gerald Ford, who replaced Richard Nixon in the White House, says he was angry and hurt that Nixon had lied to him, but he was also bothered deeply about Nixon's effect on the status of the Presidency:
>
> > What bothered me most was the nature of Nixon's departure. In the 198 years of the Republic, no President had ever resigned, and only one other Chief Executive—Andrew Johnson—had ever been the target of an impeachment effort in the Congress. But Nixon, I had to conclude, had brought his troubles upon himself. (Ford 5)

Exercise 6.7 Evaluate the punctuation and use of margins in the following in-text citations and decide whether each is *correct* or *incorrect.* Explain what is wrong with any that you decide are incorrect.

1. In his book *Blue Highways,* William Least Heat Moon describes his three-month travels along the backroads of America. He pictures a typical morning on a road in this way: Dirty and hard, the morning light could have been old concrete. Twenty-nine degrees inside. I tried to figure a way to drive down the mountain without leaving the sleeping bag. I was stiff—not from the cold so much as from having slept coiled like a grub. Creaking open and pinching toes and fingers to check for frostbite, I counted to ten (twice) before shouting and leaping for my clothes. Shouting distracts the agony." (Least Heat Moon 118).

2. During his travels, Least Heat Moon interviewed various people, including a Hopi Indian named Kendrick Fritz, who said, "To me, being Indian means being responsible to my people. Helping with the best tools. Who invented penicillin doesn't matter" (qtd. in Least Heat Moon, 119).

3. Kendrick Fritz, a Hopi Indian, answered Least Heat Moon's questions about the Hopi religion by talking of harmony, saying:

   > We don't just pray for ourselves, we pray for all things. We're famous for the Snake Dances, but a lot of people don't realize those ceremonies are prayers for rain and crops, prayers for life. We also pray for rain by sitting and thinking about rain. We sit and picture wet things like streams and clouds. It's sitting in pictures. (Qtd. in Least Heat Moon 121)

4. Least Heat Moon asked Kendrick Fritz this question, "Do you—yourself—think most whites are prejudiced against Indians?" (119). Fritz responded, "About fifty-fifty. Half show contempt because they saw a drunk squaw at the Circle K. Another half think we're noble savages." (Qtd. in Least Heat Moon 119).

5. Least Heat Moon explains in *Blue Highways* that the Hopi Indian believes in four worlds: a shadowy realm of contentment, a comfortable place of material goods, a time of worry about the past and the future, and finally a time when selfishness may block the greater vision (122).

6i   Citing Poetry

Incorporate short quotations of poetry (one or two lines) into your text. Use a slash with a space before and after to show line breaks.

> Lanier's "The Marshes of Glynn" (1878) captures the beauty of Georgia's coastal region: "Glooms of the live-oaks, beautiful-braided and woven" (1.11). When speaking of the sea, stanza 7 recounts, "Oh, what is abroad in the marsh and the terminal sea?/Somehow my soul seems suddenly free" (7.1–2).

Set off three or more lines of poetry by indenting one inch, usually two tabs on a word processor, or by centering the lines.

> The king cautions Prince Henry:
>> Thy place in council thou has rudely lost,
>> Which by thy younger brother is
>> supplied, And art almost an alien to the
>> hearts
>> Of all the court and princes of my blood.
>> (3.2.32–35)

Refer to act, scene, and lines only after you have established Shakespeare's *Henry IV, Part 1* as the central topic of your study; otherwise, write (*1H4 1.1.15–18*).

6j   Punctuating Citations

Keep page citations outside quotation marks but inside the final period (Exception: long indented quotations as shown in 6h). Use no comma between name and page within the citation (Jones 16–17 *not* Jones, 16–17). Do not use *p.* or *pp.* or *page* with the number(s).

Place commas and periods inside quotation marks unless the page citation intervenes. Place semicolons and colons outside the quotation marks.

> "Modern advertising," says Rachel Murphy, "not only creates a marketplace, it determines values." She adds, "I resist the advertiser's argument that they `awaken, not create desires'" (192).

The example above shows 1) how to interrupt a quotation to insert the speaker, 2) how to put the comma inside the quotation marks, 3) how to use single quotation marks within the regular quotation marks, and 4) how to place the period after a page citation.

When a question mark or an exclamation mark comes at the end of a quotation, keep it inside the quotation mark. Put the citation to the page number(s) after the name of the source, as shown below:

> Scientist Jonathan Roberts (54) asks, "Why do we always assume that bacteria are bad for us?"

The example below shows you how to place the page citation after a quotation and before a semicolon.

> Brian Sutton-Smith says, "Adults don't worry whether their toys are educational" (64); she adds, "Why should we always put that burden on the children?"

CHAPTER 7

Writing the Introduction

The opening section of a research paper must do more than identify the subject. A good introduction will establish the significance of an issue that warrants the reader's time as well as your efforts in preparing the paper. You should develop the four basic parts of an introduction:

- ◆ **Identify the subject**

- ◆ **Give background information**

- ◆ **Express the problem**

- ◆ **Provide a thesis statement**

By following this plan and by using the techniques described below, you can develop a complete introduction.

Checklist for the Introduction

- ◆ **Subject.** Does your introduction identify your specific topic, and then define, limit, and narrow it to one issue?

- ◆ **Background.** Does your introduction provide relevant historical data or discuss a few key sources that touch on your specific issue?

- ◆ **Problem.** Does your introduction identify a problem and explain the complications that your research paper will explore or resolve?

◆ **Thesis statement.** Does your introduction use your thesis statement within the first few paragraphs to establish the direction of the study and to point your readers toward your eventual conclusions?

How you work these essential elements into the framework of your opening will depend upon your style of writing. They need not appear in this order. Nor should you crowd all these items into a short, opening paragraph. Feel free to write a long introduction by using these additional elements:

open with a quotation

relate your topic to the well-known

review the literature

provide a brief summary

define key terms

supply data, statistics, and special evidence

take exception to critical views

The next sample of an introduction gives background information, establishes a persuasive position, reviews key literature, takes exception, gives key terms, and offers a thesis.

> Lorraine Hansberry's popular and successful *A Raisin in the Sun*, which first appeared on Broadway in 1959, is a problem play of an African American family's determination to escape a Chicago ghetto to a better life in the suburbs. There is agreement that the theme of escape explains the drama's conflict and its role in the African American movement (e.g., Oliver, Archer, and Knight, who describes the Youngers as "an entire family that has become aware of, and is determined to combat racial discrimination in a supposedly democratic land" [34]). Yet another issue lies at the heart of the drama. Hansberry develops a modern view of African American matriarchy in order to

examine both the cohesive and the conflict-producing effects it has on the individual members of the Younger family.

Avoiding certain mistakes in the opening

Avoid a purpose statement, such as "The purpose of this study is..." unless your writing reports speculative research associated with the sciences (see Chapter 12).

Avoid repetition of the title, which should appear on the first page of the text.

Avoid a quotation that has no context; that is, you have not blended it into the discussion clearly and effectively.

Avoid complex or difficult questions that may puzzle the reader. However, general rhetorical questions are acceptable.

Avoid simple dictionary definitions, such as "Webster defines a *dogmatist* as one obstinately or intolerantly devoted to his own opinions and prejudices."

7a Identifying the Topic

In writing your introduction, identify your topic as precisely as possible. You can always begin with your thesis statement, but you may want to try some of the techniques listed below to tell your readers immediately what your subject is.

- Define key terminology so that you and the readers are on common ground.

- Give an anecdote, which is a brief narrative story that shows the subject with action, dialogue, and description.

- Supply data, statistics, and special evidence to show the timely nature of the subject and its significance in our lives.

- Ask a question.

- Relate well-known facts that will appeal to the interests and knowledge of the reader, and then show your special approach.

The following passage opens a research paper with well-known facts, asks a question, and then identifies the topic:

> Children spend money just like adults. Individually, we don't have very much, like adults do, but we are a big group, and we do have an effect on the economy. Suppose we all just stopped spending money for a week? Somebody would notice. Big companies spend millions of dollars in advertising to reach us, and the advertisers always find new ways to get our money. Now companies are coming into school buildings with give-aways that carry their logos and their ads.

This next opening begins with an anecdote, and then it shifts to the topic and the thesis sentence:

> I work part-time at a local retail store. One day, while I was behind the counter near the cash register, I watched a nice-looking woman browse through the aisles. Every once in a while, she would stuff merchandise into her large handbag—a blouse, pantyhose, and several pieces of cheap costume jewelry. She was a shoplifter! I have learned that she is just one among

many. Shoplifters cause stores to raise prices to offset theft losses and the cost of security. This woman, although caught red-handed, managed to have the case dismissed. I saw her yesterday again roaming about the mall.

7b   Providing Background Information

In providing background information in your introduction, you may need to trace the historical nature of your topic, give biographical data on a person, or provide general evidence. Additionally, you may want to offer a brief summary of a novel, long poem, or other work to refresh the reader's memory about details of plot or character. You may supply a quotation by an authority to show the importance of the subject.

Avoid providing a tremendous amount of background information. Offer only the essentials necessary for the reader to understand the thesis. Later, in the body of the discussion, you may bring in additional background information when and where necessary to clarify your key points.

The example below provides background information, a quotation, and ends with a thesis statement:

> In 1941 Eudora Welty published her first book of short stories, *A Curtain of Green*. That group of stories was followed by *The Wide Net* (1943) and *The Bride of Innisfallen* (1955). Brooks and Warren view Welty's short stories as powerful reminders of the "common-sense explanations on all matters concerning life and living" (111). Each collection brought her critical acclaim, but taken together, the three volumes establish her as one of America's premier short story writers.

The next sample provides some general background information on the author, a summary of the short story, and a quotation from the story:

> Louis L'Amour is a famous writer of western stories, such as *Hondo, The Daybreakers,* and *The Lonesome Gods.* According to one source, more than one hundred thirty million copies of his books have been sold (Farrell et al. 429). His story "War Party" tells the story of Bud, a teenager who must become a man overnight after his dad gets killed. Both Bud and his mother demonstrate their courage by facing up to the father's killers as well as enduring jealous envy by their fellow travelers.

> L'Amour describes the western frontier in this way:
> > When a body crossed the Mississippi and left the settlements behind, something happened to him. The world seemed to bust wide open, and suddenly the horizons spread out and a man wasn't cramped anymore. The pinched-up villages and the narrowness of towns, all that was gone. The horizons simply exploded and rolled back into enormous distance, with nothing around but prairie and sky. (418–19)

7c   Establishing the Problem

You can establish the problem by stating one issue that you want to examine. It can be a question, an assertion, a denial, an assumption, or a challenge to existing conditions.

> Why do schools need dress codes? Nothing is gained by them. Students who want to show off will do so anyway.

The problem can raise both positive and negative issues, which means you compare and contrast the negative forces in light of the positive.

> Although Bud is the narrator and principle character in L'Amour's "War Party," the mother is the one who demonstrates great strength of character.

You might even take exception to a prevailing point of view or challenge an assumption so that readers will recognize your perspective, your argument, and your contention.

> People who say standard English is the norm for those who expect success forget that most Hispanics don't understand the Gringo meaning of "success." Law school? Dental school? There's no such dream in this world.

In the following opening, the writer begins with the thesis statement, provides a quotation, offers evidence, and ends by establishing the problem.

> Shoplifting in stores all over America has reached the point that all shoppers are suspects. Each of us is photographed, followed, watched. Susan Schneider says, "The assumption is that there are no honest shoppers" (38). People who shoplift come from all walks of life. They can be doctors, lawyers, wealthy matrons, congressmen, and even mayors. As a result, the clerks in many retail stores look at us, especially teenagers, with ill-will, not friendliness, and treat us with suspicion, not trust.

7d   Stating Your Thesis

In the introduction, you need to state your thesis. The most popular place is at the end of the introduction, but it can appear almost anywhere.

Remember the thesis statement expresses your convictions about the topic, advances your position, and limits the scope of the study. It must advance your theory about the issue and invite the reader into the argument. Here are two examples:

Sadly, the hectic pace of modern life has spilled to our roadways where the frequency and severity of road rage shows the uncaring impatience of the American driver.

Discrimination against girls and young women in the classroom, known as "shortchanging," may harm the chances of women to develop fully in the academic setting and limit their success in traditionally male-dominated fields.

Exercise 7.1 Identify the parts of the following introduction. Where is the thesis? the assertion of a problem? the identification of the topic? the background information? Is there a summary, evidence, or a quotation?

Louis L'Amour is a famous writer of western stories, such as *Hondo, The Daybreakers,* and *The Lonesome Gods.* According to one source, more than one hundred thirty million copies of his books have been sold (Farrell et al. 429). His story "War Party" tells the story of Bud, a teenager who must become a man overnight after his dad gets killed. Both Bud and his mother demonstrate their courage by facing up to the father's killers as well as enduring jealous envy by their fellow travelers.

L'Amour describes the western frontier in this way:

> When a body crossed the Mississippi and left the settlements behind, something happened to him. The world seemed to bust wide open, and suddenly the horizons spread out and a man wasn't cramped anymore. The pinched-up villages and the narrowness of towns, all that was gone. The horizons simply exploded and rolled back into enormous distance, with nothing around but prairie and sky. (418–19)

People had to grow up fast on the frontier. Although Bud is the narrator and principal character, the mother is the one who demonstrates great strength. So "War Party" is not Bud's story, although he tells it. The true heroine is Bud's mother.

 Exercise 7.2 Begin drafting your own introduction by following the steps below.

1. Identify the topic.

2. Provide some background information.

3. Furnish a good quotation from the sources.

4. Express the problem.

5. State your thesis.

CHAPTER 8

Writing the Body of the Research Paper

The body of the research paper should develop the major issues of your outline. It body should explore at least two major issues but may examine three or more. The body of the paper should identify your major areas of interest and explore each one with a variety of techniques, as explained in this chapter.

Checklist for the Body of the Paper

◆ **Analysis.** Classify the major issues of the study and provide causal analysis or process analysis of each.

◆ **Presentation.** Provide well-reasoned statements in topic sentences at the beginning of your paragraphs.

◆ **Defense.** Supply evidence of support with proper documentation. Offer a variety of development to compare, show process, narrate the history of the subject, or show causes. These techniques are explained in this chapter.

The following paragraphs demonstrate the use of several techniques: a presentation of the problem and a defense of the statement with the citation of a source, comparison, causal analysis, definition, and process analysis.

> To burn or not to burn the natural forests in the national parks is the question. The pyrophobic public voices its protests while environmentalists praise the rejuvenating effects of a good forest fire. It is difficult to convince people that not all fire is bad. The public has visions of Smokey the Bear campaigns and mental images of the forest's inhabitants fleeing the roaring flames. Chris Bolgiano explains that federal policy evolved slowly "from the basic impulse to douse all fires immediately to a sophisticated decision matrix based on the functions of any given unit of land" (23). Bolgiano explains, "timber production, grazing, recreation, and wilderness preservation elicit different fire-management approaches" (23).

8a   Planning and Outlining the Body

Here is a sample plan for one student's paper on Martin Luther King, Jr. The writer used it as a framework for the body of her paper.

II. The Body

A. Major issue one: Civil Rights Movement

1. Successful leadership of the "Montgomery Bus Boycott"

2. "I Have a Dream" speech

B. Major issue two: preoccupation with death

1. deep apprehensions about going to Washington

2. his speech made on April 3

C. Major issue three: commitment to his cause

1. poor people's campaign and the danger of it

2. arrested and jailed several times during the protest

This plan enabled the writer to develop several paragraphs on the key discoveries of her investigation. The material supported her introduction and pointed forward to a conclusion. You can add substance to the body of your paper by using an outline.

8b Building the Body

As with the introduction, you should pick and choose your techniques. Some techniques will trace the issues and events, others will compare, and still others will classify and analyze.

Chronology

Use **chronology** to trace historical events and to explain a sequence by time. You may need to discuss the causes or consequences of certain events.

> Gaining courage and strength to face the frontier is not an overnight affair. Bud and his mother in L'Amour's "War Party" cross the Mississippi and enter areas where "the horizons simply exploded and rolled back into enormous distance, with nothing around but prairie and sky" (419). Life will not be easy, and they will face many hardships. Early on, Bud's father is killed, but Bud and his mother push forward.

Keep the plot summary short and relate it to your thesis, as shown by the first sentence of the passage above. Do not allow plot summary to extend beyond one paragraph because you may retell the entire story. Your task is to make a point, not to retell the story.

Comparison and contrast

Employ **comparison** and **contrast** to show the two sides of a subject, to compare two characters, to compare the past with the present, or to compare positive and negative issues.

> Bud is still a child, but he is tough and smart. He kills a buffalo, and later on he kills an antelope on the run. He knows when to remain silent and when to speak boldly. However, his mother is the heroine of the story. She is the one who decides to continue west after her husband, Bud's father, has been killed. In fact, she killed the man who sent the fatal arrow into her husband. She faces up to Mr. Buchanan, who wanted her to turn back. She ignores the grumbling of fellow travelers. She makes a home.

Cause and effect

Use **cause** and **effect** to develop the reasons for a circumstance and/or to examine the consequences.

> Sometimes a child is only as strong as adults will allow. In "War Party," Bud rises to a new level because his mother lets it happen. She tells Buchanan, "I have my man. Bud is almost thirteen and accepts responsibility. I could ask for no better man" (420). Bud rewards her confidence at the end of the story by confronting Buchanan: "Mr. Buchanan, I may be little and may be a fool, but this here rifle doesn't care who pulls its trigger" (427).

Classify and analyze

Classify and **analyze** the various causes, reasons, and consequences of the issues. Spend some time discussing the various items and develop each one in support of the thesis statement.

> Was Bud's mother in "War Party" a Dakota Indian? She spoke the people's language and was able to calm the Dakota chief and his warriors. She saved the wagon train, but the people were suspicious. How did

she know the language? Some of them wanted to kick her off the wagon train. As it turned out, she was not an Indian at all. She had grown up playing with Dakota youngsters in Minnesota. At a crucial moment, she drew upon that knowledge to save her family.

Developing a paragraph or two on each method of development is one way to build the body of your paper. Write a comparison paragraph, classify and analyze one or two issues, then pose a question and answer it. Sooner than you think, you will draft the body of your paper.

Definition

Use **definition** to expand upon a complex subject.

> For some people, the western frontier was an opportunity, for some it was challenge, and for others it was dangerous territory best avoided. To Bud in "War Party," the frontier was adventure. To his mother, it would be "home." Bud thought home was something they had left. His mother explained, "Home is where we're going now, and we'll know it when we find it" (420).

Process analysis

Draft a **process analysis** paragraph that offers a stage-by-stage explanation of the steps necessary to achieve a desired end.

> For the frontier hero, the first stage is making the decision to cross the Mississippi. The second stage is finding the courage to continue the quest against boredom, danger, poor weather, and lack of supplies. The third stage is overcoming the fear of death by accident, drowning, trampling, or others. The fourth stage, and the most dangerous, is facing the envy and jealousy of companions and fellow travelers.

Question and answer

Frame a **question** and **answer** it with specific details and evidence.

> Were early frontiersmen prejudiced in their treatment of women? L'Amour's story says "yes." One of the rules of the wagon train demonstrates the prejudice: "There has to be a man with every wagon" (420). A few travelers condemned Bud's mother for her outspoken ways. Later, when she confronted the Dakota chief, many people thought she was out of place because confronting an Indian was a man's job. They even suspected that Mrs. Miles was an Indian herself.

Evidence from the source material

Cite the various authorities on the subject. Provide quotations, paraphrases, and summaries in support of your topic sentences.

> Louis L'Amour acquired his knowledge from people who lived the frontier life, including one old man who had been a captive of the Apaches and raised in his childhood with them (CB 203). Having used the old man as a reference source, L'Amour says, "He was a man who knew all about the Apaches, how they lived, how they worked, how they fought" (qtd. in CB 203). L'Amour adds, "In much of his thinking, he was still an Apache."

There is no reason to provide a page citation for the final quotation because it obviously came from the same source. Cite every source, but do not needlessly clutter your text with citations when the reference is clear to the reader.

Other methods

There are several other methods for developing paragraphs, such as description, statistics, symbolism, point of view, scientific evidence, history, character, and setting. You must make the choices, basing your decision on your subject and your notes.

8c Writing Topic Sentences

Paragraphs of a research paper need substance. The topic sentence of each paragraph sets the stage for full development of ideas and issues. Here are a few suggestions:

1. Write a topic sentence that requires you to classify and explain several stages of development.

   The pageantry of high school football includes far more than the game itself.

2. Use a question as the topic sentence.

   How does the average citizen contribute to the build-up of acid rain?

3. Write a topic sentence that allows you to expand with chronological information.

   Most amphibians experience a metamorphosis — a change in their bodies — as they grow and develop.

4. Write a topic sentence that allows you to expand with description.

   The turtle's shell is a burdensome shield.

5. Write a topic sentence that challenges an assumption and requires well-developed support.

   The year 2000 was not merely the year of the disputed election.

6. Write a topic sentence that introduces the scholarship on the subject.

Several critics have examined Hawthorne's imagery of darkness and gloom.

7. Write a topic sentence that is broad enough to demand specific information.

Humans, as well as animals, learn by association.

Topic Sentence #7 is reprinted below, followed by a paragraph that develops it. Notice how this topic sentence invites readers into the discussion of learning, then expands the idea with examples of both human and animal behavior.

Humans, as well as animals, learn by association. We respond to various impulses and preferences. A cat hears the electric can opener and comes running to the kitchen, expecting to be fed. A basketball player hears a referee's whistle and groans, expecting to be called for committing a foul. We learn by associating the sound to a specific result. "One kind of learning by association results in conditioned response—a desired response to an unusual stimulus" (Balzar et al. 368). Pavlov's experiments many years ago proved that dogs could learn a conditioned response. We also learn by positive reinforcement and by rewards, as demonstrated by well-behaved children just before Christmas or by performing bears at a circus.

8d   Writing Paragraphs

Give readers sufficient evidence to support each topic sentence. The paragraphs in the body of a research paper should be at least one-half page in length. You can do this only by writing good topic sentences and by developing them with the techniques explained in 8c.

If shoplifters are looting retail stores in ever larger numbers, who pays? Well, the bill comes to you and me, the honest shoppers who must make up the difference. We have to pay not only for shoplifting but for the cost of security measures. Jack Fraser, a retail executive, states: "Stores are losing 1.94 percent of sales per year—and that doesn't even include the expense of maintaining the security staff and equipment. That's a lot of cash. It cuts into profits" (qtd. in Schneider 38).

This writer uses a question-answer sequence to build the paragraph by posing the question, "Who pays?" The writer then answers it, "consumers pay," and defends that answer with a quotation from an authority on the subject.

Almost every paragraph you write in the body of the research paper is, in one way or another, explanatory. You must state your position in a good topic sentence and then list and evaluate your evidence.

Notice how the following writer defends a topic sentence with specific details. The accumulation of evidence builds a paragraph of substance.

Let the real world into the public schools. Many companies have found it advantageous to furnish a satellite dish for every school in a school system and a television set for every classroom. We should use them. They bring PBS programs and other news and features to the students. We should use videotapes, camcorders, audio cassettes with "walkmen," electronic keyboards, and computers. Some students have better electronic equipment at home in their bedrooms than in their schools. A teacher, a desk, and a book are not enough anymore. Computer corporations have made gifts of computers to schools for many years. They had a profit motive, but so what? Look at the alternative—no computers at all in the schools.

Exercise 8.1 Rather than merely writing a paragraph as it occurs to you, take the time to list the technique(s) that you will use to build the paragraph. Remember, your outline will not always reveal the best technique for drafting a paragraph. A paragraph plan reads like this:

> I'm going to list the Tennessee battles of General Ulysses Grant to show his progressive fulfillment of a major plan. The paragraph will help defend the topic sentence about Grant as both a patient and a determined commander.

> I am going to classify certain educational toys for preschool children to examine and evaluate their effectiveness in later paragraphs.

> Write the technique(s) you will use for developing one paragraph of your body.

 Exercise 8.2 Using the technique(s) from Exercise 8.1, build a paragraph.

CHAPTER 9

Writing the Conclusion

The conclusion of a research paper reaffirms the thesis statement, discusses the issues, and reaches a final judgment. The conclusion is not a summary. It is a belief based on your reasoning and based on the evidence you have accumulated. This is the place to share with readers the conclusions you have reached because of your research.

9a   Writing a Conclusion

The nature of the study can dictate your use of the following items. Use several of the following techniques to build a conclusion of substance.

◆ Reaffirm the topic and restate your thesis to express your primary ideas.

> Shoplifting by a few people casts a shadow on every man, woman, and child who enters a retail store. In a small convenience store as well as a huge department store every person is a potential customer. Unfortunately, every customer is also a potential shoplifter in the eyes of the clerks. We are suspects no matter how noble we may be. The customer is no longer right.

◆ Supply a quotation or two in defense of your position.

> Schneider says, "While the incidence of other larcenies has dropped, the FBI reported that shoplifting rose 33 percent between 1995 and 1999 and that about a million shoplifters are arrested every year" (38). The evidence only gets worse. Schneider adds, "For every person who gets caught, ten get away" (19).

◆ Conclude with an anecdote, which is a brief narrative story that will show the subject with action, dialogue, and description.

> Jeremy Thornton, who operates a small neighborhood grocery store, relates one of his experiences:
>
>> I caught a 10-year-old girl putting candy inside her dress. What to do? She denied it, and I can't search her. So I let her go. Ten minutes later her mother comes in, busts me in the mouth, and calls me a dirty old man. I'm only 45, but I'm ready to lock the doors and retire (qtd. in Rover 34–35).
>
> No wonder owners and store clerks like Thornton view every shopper with suspicion, not trust, and at times with open hostility rather than old-fashioned courtesy.

◆ Take exception to a prevailing point of view or challenge an assumption so that readers will recognize your perspective, your argument, or your contention.

> Like other people, I resent being treated as a thief, being televised, watched, and forced to walk through detectors when I leave a store. However, after investigating the facts, I understand why.

◆ Discuss the data, statistics, and special evidence to show their relevance to your final statements.

> Jack Fraser, a retail executive, states: "Stores are losing 1.94 percent of sales per year—and that doesn't even include the expense of maintaining the security staff and equipment" (qtd. in Schneider 38).

◆ Compare past events to the present situation, compare prior findings to the present evidence, or compare outdated ideas in light of contemporary thinking.

> Burglary during hours when retail stores are closed is minor in comparison with shoplifting thefts when stores are open. Amazing as it seems, thieves would rather operate during daylight hours than break into the store at night.

◆ Focus on the central figure to discuss the contributions made by a novelist, a political figure, or a military hero. Use this technique with biographies and literary studies.

> L'Amour is noted as a writer of the western frontier, and people probably think of him as a rugged male like Mr. Buchanan in "War Party." However, L'Amour demonstrates an understanding of women. He shows that they can be tough and that they have visions for the future. Mrs. Miles is not a feminist by modern standards, but she manages well in a man's world. Thus, L'Amour balances the rugged West with a blend of men *and* women.

Checklist for the Conclusion

◆ **Thesis.** Reaffirm the thesis statement and the central mission of your study. If appropriate, give a statement in support or nonsupport of an original idea or hypothesis.

◆ **Judgments.** Discuss and interpret the findings. Give answers. Now is the time to draw inferences, to emphasize a theory, and to find relevance in the details of the results.

◆ **Directives.** Based on the theoretical implications of the study, offer suggestions for action and for new research.

Exercise 9.1 Using the passage below, identify at least five of these techniques used in developing the conclusion: 1) reaffirms the topic, 2) uses a quotation from the sources, 3) takes exception to a prevailing point of view and challenges an assumption, 4) uses a question-and-answer sequence, 5) cites facts and evidence, and 6) reaches a final judgment.

In many cases, television is simply "junk food" (Fransecky 117), and excessive viewing distracts us from other, worthwhile activities. Yet television can and does bring cultural programs and some of our best literature into homes and schools. Can television always be viewed as an unpleasant appliance with little or no cultural value? It can, according to the evidence, improve children's vocabularies, encourage their reading, and inspire their writing. Television and school should not be antagonists. They should complement one another within the traditional classroom curriculum, finding harmony with the preschool television curriculum.

9b   Avoiding Certain Mistakes in the Conclusion

Your conclusion should carry your reader to a new level of perception about the topic. A summary of what you have said in the paper is not satisfactory. After all, the reader will hardly need reminding of things just read. Therefore, use a combination of the techniques explained in section 9a. Note the manner in which this next conclusion uses these techniques. It reaffirms the topic and thesis, cites specific facts, uses a paraphrase from an authority, challenges the assumption that school must be serious, compares outdated ideas in light of contemporary thinking, and reaches a final conclusion.

> In the traditional patriarchal family, the child was legal property of the parents. However, the idea that children are the property of the parents and, therefore, may receive whatever punishment seems necessary, no longer holds true. Social organizations and governmental agencies now help young victims in their search for preventive measures. Contrary to the past, children today have rights, too!

Avoid afterthoughts or additional ideas. The conclusion is the time to end the paper, not begin a new thought. If new ideas occur to you as you write your conclusion, do not ignore them. Explore them fully in the context of your thesis and consider adding them to the body of your paper or slightly modifying your thesis.

Avoid the use of "thus," "in conclusion," or "finally" at the beginning of the last paragraph. Readers will be able to see the end of the paper.

Avoid ending the paper without a sense of closure.

Avoid questions that raise new issues. However, rhetorical questions that restate the issues are acceptable.

Exercise 9.2 Plan your own conclusion. Describe the methods that might help you write an effective conclusion. An example follows:

My conclusion about teenage suicide will do these things: restate my thesis, quote George Goodwin, take exception to his point of view, cite again my collected evidence from personal interviews, and end with the final moments of one teenager's losing struggle to be heard.

Exercise 9.3 Begin drafting your own conclusion by making notes. Remember to share with the reader your final judgment about the subject instead of just repeating what you have already said in the introduction or the body.

CHAPTER 10

Works Cited

A bibliography is a list of books and articles about a particular subject. Written as a Works Cited page, the bibliography serves others who might wish to read further in the literature. For your Works Cited page prepare a bibliographic entry for each source cited in your paper.

In preparing this page, align the first line of each source flush with the left margin and indent succeeding lines five spaces. Double-space throughout. Do not list sources that you skimmed but did not use in the paper.

10a Bibliographic Form — Books

Use this order: 1) author(s), 2) title, 3) a specific volume number, 4) editor(s), 5) edition other than the first, 6) number of volumes if more than one, 7) place of publication, 8) publisher (abbreviated), 9) date, and 10) page. List items essential for finding the source.

Abbreviate the names of the publishers. Use this list as a guide:

Addison (Addison Wesley Longman)
Norton (W. W. Norton and Company)
Prentice (Prentice-Hall)
Allyn (Allyn and Bacon, Inc.)
Holt (Holt, Rinehart, and Winston, Inc.)

Oxford UP (Oxford University Press)
U of Chicago P (University of Chicago Press)

Use the following examples as models.

Author

McMillan, Terry. *A Day Late and a Dollar Short*. New York: Viking, 2001.

Authors, two and edition

Korper, Steffano, and Juanita Ellis. *The E-Commerce Book*. 2nd ed. San Diego: Academic Press, 2001.

Authors, more than three

Use "et al.," which means "and others," or list all the authors.

Lewis, Laurel J., et al. *Linear Systems Analysis*. New York: McGraw, 2000.

Author, two works by the same author

Alphabetize the entries by titles and use three hyphens to signal repetition of the same author.

Irving, John. *The Cider House Rules*. New York: Ballantine, 1985.

– – –. *A Prayer for Owen Meany*. New York: Ballantine, 1985.

Anthology, textbook, other edited works

Crotty, Patrick, ed. *Modern Irish Poetry*. Belfast: Blackstaff, 1995.

If you cite one work from an anthology, use this form:

Heaney, Seamus. "The Birthplace." *Modern Irish Poetry*. Ed. Patrick Crotty. Belfast: Blackstaff, 1995. 120–21.

Author, corporation, or institution

A corporate author can be an association, a committee, or any group or institution when the title page does not identify the names of the members. List a committee or council as the author even when the organization is also the publisher, as in this example:

Association for Supervision and Curriculum Development. *Curriculum Update.* Alexandria, VA: ASCD, 2000.

The Bible

Do not underscore or italicize the word *Bible* or the books of the Bible. Common editions need no publication information. Underscore or italicize special editions of the Bible.

The Bible. Revised Standard Version.

The New Open Bible. New Living Translation. Nashville: Thomas Nelson, 1998.

Encyclopedias, alphabetized works, and biographical dictionaries

Well-known works need only the edition and the year of publication. If no author is listed, begin with the title of the article:

Ward, Norman. "Saskatchewan." *Encyclopedia Americana.* 1998 ed.

"Astronaut." *The American Heritage Dictionary of the English Language.* 3rd ed. 1996.

Special edition of a novel

Baum, L. Frank. *The Wizard of Oz.* Centennial Edition. Ed. Michael P. Hearn. New York: Norton, 2000.

Volumes, one of several volumes

Jackson, Andrew. *The Papers of Andrew Jackson: 1770–1803.* Vol. 1. Ed. Sam B. Smith and Harriet C. Owsley. 4 vols. Knoxville: U of Tennessee P, 1980.

10b Bibliographic Form — Periodicals

Use this order for writing a bibliographic entry for articles found in magazines, journals, and newspapers: 1) author(s), 2) title of the article within quotation marks, 3) name of the magazine, journal, or newspaper underlined, 4) specific date, 5) inclusive page numbers (but use a "+" with the opening page (14+) if advertising pages intervene or if the article skips to the back pages of the magazine.

Author

Bertolucci, Jeff. "So Long, Shrink-Wrap?" *PC World* Feb. 2001: 110–20.

Authors, two

Sawhney, Mohanbir, and Deval Parikh. "Where Value Lives in a Networked World." *Harvard Business Review* Jan. 2001: 79–86.

Author, not listed

"Facing a Dilemma at Justice." *Newsweek* 15 Jan. 2001: 6.

Interview, published

Jackson, Samuel L. Interview. *Madison* July/Aug. 2000: 94–101.

Journal article

Wood, Susan N. "Bringing Us the Way to Know: The Novels of Gary Paulsen." *English Journal* 90.3 (Jan. 2001): 67–72.

Journal article, all issues for a year numbered continuously

> Ochoa, Gian-Carlo, et al. "A Functional Link Between Dynamin and Actin Cytoskeleton at Podosomes." *Journal of Cell Biology* 150 (2000): 377–90.

Many journals page continuously through all issues of an entire year. Thus, the volume number, year, and pages are sufficient for locating a journal article. If a journal does page anew, provide the issue number (for example, "66.2").

Newspaper

Include the section with the page number when citing a newspaper article.

> Weise, Elizabeth. "'It Makes for Lots of Speculation." *USA Today* 15 Jan. 2001: 1D.

Review article

> Brown, Bruce, and Marge Brown. "AOL Home Extensions." Rev. of *Gateway Connected Touch Pad. PC Magazine* 6 Feb. 2001: 30.

10c Bibliographic Form — Electronic Sources

Rapidly changing technology makes it possible to access a tremendous number of sources from the Internet, E-mail, and CD-ROM disks. The Internet, in particular, opens a broad array of information from millions of sources. Remember that Web sites change and can become unavailable.

It is essential that you include enough information in your bibliographic citations so that a reader can find your source. Use these items as appropriate to the source: 1) author/editor name; 2) title of the article in quotation marks, or the title of a posting to a discussion list or forum, followed by the words *Online posting*, followed by a period; 3) name of the book, journal, or complete work, italicized or underlined; 4) publication information — place, publisher, and date for books, volume and year of a journal, exact date of a magazine, date and description for government documents; 5) name of the sponsoring institution or organization, if available; 6) date of your access, not followed by a comma or a period; 7) URL (Uniform Resource Locator), in angle brackets, followed by a period.

Do not include page numbers unless the Internet article shows original page numbers from the printed version of the journal or magazine. Do not include the total number of paragraphs or specific paragraph numbers unless the original Internet article has provided them.

Article online, no author

"People: Your Greatest Asset." *Human Resources*. 15 July 1999. 14 Sept. 2000 <http://netscape/business/humanresources/>.

E-mail

Crimmins, Gary. "Writing Analysis." E-mail to the author. 20 May, 2001.

Encyclopedia

Encyclopedia Britannica Online. Vers. 99.1. 1994–1999. Encyclopedia Britannica. 19 Aug. 2001 <http://www.eb.com/>.

Government document

United States. Cong. Senate. *Superfund Cleanup
Acceleration Act of 1997.* 21 Jan. 1997. 105th Cong.
Senate Bill 8. 4 March 2001.
<http.thomas.loc.gov/egibin/query/2/C105:S.8:>.

Home page for a web site

Dawe, James. *Jane Austen Page.* 15 May 2001
<http://nyquiet.ee.ualberta.ca/~dawe/austen.html>.

Journal article, reproduced online

Miller, B. A., N. J. Smyth, and P. J. Mudar. "Mothers'
Alcohol and Other Drug Problems and Their
Punitiveness toward Their Children." *Journal of Studies
on Alcohol* 60 (1999): 632–42. 28 Sept. 2000
<http://www.ncbi.nlm.hih.gov.htbin>.

Magazine article online

Carney, Dan, Mike France, and Spencer E. Ante. "Web
Access Is Becoming a Dicey Issue for Industry and
Regulators." *BusinessWeek Online* 31 July 2000. 2
Aug. 2000 <http://www.businessweek.com/
2000/00_31>.

Miscellaneous Internet sources

List the type of work for such items as a cartoon,
map, chart, or advertisement as shown in this
example:

"U.S. Territorial Map 1870." *American Historical Atlas:
U.S. Territorial Maps 1775–1920.* U of Virginia Lib.
17 June 1996. 25 Oct. 2000 <http//xroals.Virginia.edu/
~map/TERRITORY/187omdp.html>.

Newspaper article online

Firestone, David. "Anonymous Louisiana Slaves Regain
Identity." *New York Times on the Web* 30 July 2000. 8
Aug. 2000 <http://www.nytimes.com/
library/national/073000a-slaves.html>.

Poem or story online

Keats, John. "Ode on a Grecian Urn." *Poetical Works.*
1884. *Project Bartleby.* 2000 Great Books Online. 8
March 2001 <http://www.bartleby.edu/
126/41.html>.

Report online

Watkins, R.E. "An Historical Review of the Role and Practice
of Psychology in the Field of Corrections." Report No.
R-29. Correctional Service of Canada. 1992. 3 May
2001 <http://www.csc-scc.gc.ca/crd/reports/r28e/
r28e/htm>.

10d Bibliographic Form — CD-ROM Sources

Full-text articles are available on CD-ROM from
national distributors, such as Information Access
Company (*InfoTrac*), UMI-Proquest (*Proquest*),
Silverplatter, or *SIRS* CD-ROM Information
Systems.

DePalma, Antony. "Mexicans Renew Their Pact on the
Economy, Retaining the Emphasis on Stability." *New
York Times* 25 Sept. 1994: 4. *New York Times Ondisc.*
CD-ROM. UMI-Proquest. Jan. 2001.

"Abolitionist Movement." *Compton's Interactive
Encyclopedia.* CD-ROM. Softkey Multimedia. 1996.

Poe, Edgar Allan. "Fall of the House of Usher." *Electronic
Classical Library.* CD-ROM. Garden Grove, CA: World
Library, 1999.

10e Bibliographic Form — Other Sources

Use the examples below for bibliographic entries
written for the variety of sources listed below. Be

sure to provide enough information so that readers can understand the nature of the source.

Advertisement

"Yahoo! Travel." Advertising page. *Trips*. Feb. 2001: 17.

Art, a reproduction in a book

Raphael. *School of Athens*. 1510–1511. The Vatican, Rome. *The World Book Encyclopedia*. 2000 ed.

Broadcast interview

Cooper, John M. "Woodrow Wilson," Interview. *American Presidents*. C-SPAN2. 13 Sept. 1999.

Bulletin

Safety Tips for Travelers. Bulletin 11B. Philadelphia: International SOS, 2001.

Cassette tapes

Drake, Robert. "Eudora Welty's 'A Worn Path' as a Roadmap of Southern Life." Lecture on cassette tape. Knoxville: U of Tennessee, 2000.

Computer software

New Millennium World Atlas. Computer software. Skokie, IL: Rand McNally, 2000.

Conference proceedings

Gunawan, Dani, and Husen Beshir, eds. *Technology and Persons with Disabilities*. Center on Disabilities. Proceedings of the Sixteenth Annual Conference. Mar. 19–24. California State U., Northridge. Northridge, CA: California State UP, 2001.

Government document

Provide government, body, subsidiary body, title, identifying numbers, and publication facts for government documents.

United States. Cong. House. Committee on Veterans Affairs. *Veterans Claims Assistance Act of 2000.* 106th Cong., H6786-90. Washington, DC: GPO, 2000.

Film or video recording

Cite title, director, distributor, and year.

The Love Letter. Dir. Peter Ho-Sun Chan. DVD. Dreamworks Home Entertainment, 1999.

Interview

For an interview that you conduct, name the person interviewed, the type of interview (e.g., telephone interview, personal interview, e-mail interview), and the date.

Kraak, Phillip. Telephone interview. 18 Jan. 2001.

Letter, personal

Noell, Shannon. Letter to the author. 5 Mar. 2001.

Letter, published

Duke, Jas W. Letter from Military Prison, Rock Island Illinois. 31 Aug. 1864. *The Civil War: Unstilled Voices.* By Chuck Lawliss. New York: Crown, 1999.

Map

U.S. Dept. of Agriculture. *County Boundaries.* United States. Map ID: 2144. Washington, DC: USDA, January 2001.

Miscellaneous materials (program, leaflet, poster, announcement)

"Earth Day 2000." Poster. Milwaukee. 22 Apr. 2000.

Pamphlet

Treat pamphlets as you would a book.

Tubbs, Robert. *Recycling Works!* Bismarck, ND: North Dakota Dept. of Health, 1999.

Recording

Indicate the medium (e.g., audio cassette, audiotape, or LP [long-playing record]).

Yeats, William Butler. "Adam's Curse." *Literature Aloud.* Narr. by Julian Sands. Compact Disc. Boston: Bedford/St. Martin's, 2000.

Tables, illustrations, charts, or graphs

Tables or illustrations of any kind published within works need a label (e.g., chart, table, figure, or photograph):

O'Neill, June E. "Revenues, by Source, as a Percentage of GDP Fiscal Years 1940–1999." Figure 5. *Policy Review* 101 (June - July 2000): 12.

Television

"Women & Fibroids." Narr. Jovita Moore. *Action News.* WATC, Atlanta. 8 Aug. 2000.

Unpublished paper

Strange, Yolanda. "Heart Lines and Life Lines: Hearing the Warnings of Teen Suicide." Unpublished paper. Manhattan, KS, 2000.

Videotape

From Earth to the Moon. Dir. Tom Hanks. Documentary. HBO Video, 1998.

Exercise 10.1 Unscramble each of the following entries and write a correct bibliographic entry for each one.

1. Interview. April 5, 2001. Dayton, Ohio. Jane Pullet, county historian.

2. *Encyclopedia Americana.* "Communication Satellite." 2000 edition.

3. *USA Today.* Mary Beth Marklein, author. "Colleges Help Newcomers Find the Way." Wednesday, May 19, 2001, page 9A.

4. *Three Famous Short Novels* by William Faulkner published in 1942 by Vintage Books in New York.

5. *Correspondence of Andrew Jackson* by Andrew Jackson. Volume 1 of 2 volumes. Edited by J. S. Bassett. Published in Washington, D.C., by Carnegie Institution of Washington, 1926.

10f Preparing a Works Cited Page

A Works Cited page must list each source that you cite in your text, including any references in footnotes, figures, tables, or appendices. If you list sources that you did not cite in the text, call the list Works Consulted.

Your working bibliography that you began in Chapter 2 will provide the basis for your list if you have kept your entries up-to-date. Arrange the list in alphabetical order by the last name of the author. Double-space throughout. When no author is listed, alphabetize by the first important word of the title. Use three hyphens to replace the name of a repeated source. Set the title *Works Cited* one inch down from the top of the sheet and double-space between it and the first entry. A short Works Cited page is shown next. (See another example on page 157.)

Works Cited

Abbott, Ellen. "29 Minute Pyramid." *The Treading Workout Workbook*. 1999. 12 May 2001 <http://www.treading.com/29pyr.html>.

"Fitness Tip — The Walking Workout." 3 Jan. 2001. 27 Jan. 2001 <http://ideafit.com/ftwalking.htm>.

Jacobson, Jake. *Healthwalk to Fitness*. Levittown, NY: Heartfit, 1999.

Kortge, Carolyn S. *The Spirited Walker*. San Francisco: Harper, 1998.

– – –. *Steps to Fitness*. Video. Wichita, KS: Ctr. Improvement of Human Functioning, 2000.

"Should You Add Weights to Your Walking Workout?" 25 July 2000. 27 Jan. 2001 <http://www.efit.com/servlet/article/5642.html>.

As a researcher, you have an ethical obligation to list each source cited in your text or in any content note. You need not list sources consulted but not used. A Works Cited list should not be padded with unused books and articles.

Exercise 10.2 Write an alphabetical list of your sources. Submit it to your instructor for review, if requested to do so. Then, use it to frame your final Works Cited page.

CHAPTER 11

Preparing the Final Paper

After completing the initial draft of your paper, you face the important task of turning the rough copy into a finished paper. For the final draft, you will need to conform to standards that present the material in a clear and logical manner. In this chapter, you will learn to format the paper according to the style of the Modern Language Association (MLA).

- **Formatting** means preparing the presentation of your paper according to page placement, spacing, and content.

- **Revising** means to altering, amending, and improving the entire paper.

- **Editing** means preparing the draft for final writing by checking style, word choice, and grammar.

- **Proofreading** means examining the final manuscript to spot any last-minute errors.

11a Formatting the Paper

In every case, you should:

Double-space all lines.

Maintain a one-inch margin on each edge of the sheet.

Indent paragraphs five spaces.

Indent long quotations of four lines or more one inch or ten spaces. Single space the quotation.

Indent poetry quotations of three lines or more one inch, ten spaces, or center the lines of poetry evenly within your margins.

Indent the second and succeeding lines of the bibliographic entries five spaces. The first line is flush left.

Center your title on the first page and center the words Works Cited on the last page.

Put your last name with the page number in the upper-right corner of every page.

List your name and course description on the opening page

You do not need a separate title page. Instead, you can place the course information flush left at the top of your opening page. List your full name, the teacher's name, and the date. If you *do* write a separate title page, omit this course information from your opening page.

Shannon O'Malley
Mrs. Broadbent
Sophomore English
17 May 2001

"War Party" and L'Amour's
View of Women

Writing a title page

Center the information on a title page, as shown below. Use an inverted pyramid order for the title by placing the longest line first. Follow the title with your name, your teacher's name, and the date. You may add the course title and name of the school. Do not underline the title, place it within quotation marks, or decorate the title with artwork. Following is a sample title page:

"War Party" and L'Amour's View of Women

Shannon O'Malley

**Mrs. Broadbent
Sophomore English
Blakely High School**

May 17, 2001

Writing the research paper on a computer

Use the computer's ability to generate a polished paper. You can store and retrieve your notes and drafts, revise by moving blocks of material from one place to the next, and edit quickly on a monitor screen. After keyboarding the paper one time, you can get multiple printouts as you revise and proofread. Remember to preserve all your notes and rough drafts. The teacher may want to see how the paper grew from your notes and the rough draft.

With some computers you can create graphic designs, show italic typeface rather than underlining, and even print with various fonts, such as Helvetica or Times Roman.

Take advantage of the computer's special features to edit the paper. If software is available to check your spelling, your grammar, and your style, use it.

11b Revising the Paper

It is important to make "global" revisions of your paper. For this task, you must be willing to reword, rearrange, and rework the text of the paper.

Begin by examining your **introduction** for a thesis that gives a clear direction or plan of development and a sense of your involvement with the reader. See Chapter 7 for additional tips and guidelines about the opening section for your paper.

Examine the **body** of the paper for a clear sequence of major statements that provide appropriate and effective evidence to support your key ideas. Look for clear transitions that move the reader effectively from one block of material to another. See Chapter 8 for more advice for developing the major text of your project.

Examine the ending of the paper for a **conclusion** that is drawn from the evidence given in the body of the paper. The conclusion should evolve logically from the key points made in the paper and clearly convey your position and interpretation. See Chapter 9 for a complete discussion of the conclusion.

Work your way through your entire paper again and again. Keep in mind that even the best of writers often revise various versions of their drafts several times.

11c Editing the Paper

Read through your paper to study your sentence structure and word choices. Follow the examples below for making the proper corrections in your paper:

◆ Cut phrases and sentences that do not advance your main ideas or that merely repeat what your sources have already stated.

Poor: One critic calls television "junk food" (Fransecky 77). I also think television is junk food. I think watching television takes time away from other things.

Better: Television critic Jewis Fransecky views much of what appears on television as "junk food" (77). In truth, television viewing keeps us from many worthwhile activities.

◆ Look for ways to change *to be* verbs, such as *is, are,* and *was,* to stronger action verbs.

Poor: Television is a hindrance because it does not encourage children's reading and writing.

Better: Television hinders the reading and writing skills of school-age children.

◆ Try to convert passive structures to active ones.

Poor: Television was never intended to act as a babysitter for pre-school children.

Better: Television may delay the development of pre-school children.

◆ Confirm that your paraphrases and quotations flow smoothly within your text.

Poor: Mark Aldridge thinks that television slows reading skills. "Children who are plopped in front of a television set are deprived of the necessary skills needed for reading comprehension (19). This affects pre-school children.

Better: Mark Aldridge believes that pre-school children "plopped in front of a television set are deprived of the necessary skills needed for reading comprehension" (19).

◆ Check your spelling.

Poor: Parents must bee proactive in providing a nurturing environment for there children.

Better: Parents must be proactive in providing a nurturing environment for *their* children.

11d Avoiding Discriminatory Language

You must exercise caution against words that may stereotype any person, regardless of gender, race, nationality, creed, age, or disability. If your writing is not precise, readers might make mistaken assumptions about your subject. To many people, a doctor or governor may bring to mind a white male, while a similar reference to a teacher or homemaker may bring to mind a woman. In truth, no characteristic should be assumed for all members of a group. The following are some guidelines to help you avoid discriminatory language:

Age

Review the accuracy of your statements when referring to age.

Discriminatory: Many elderly suffer senility.

Avoid *elderly* as a noun; use *older persons. Dementia* is preferred over the word *senility.*

Gender

Gender is a matter of our culture that identifies men and women within their social groups. *Sex* tends to be a biological factor. Use plural subjects so that nonspecific, plural pronouns are grammatically correct. For example, indicate that technicians, in general, maintain *their* own equipment. Some people now use a plural pronoun with the singular *everybody, everyone, anybody, anyone,* and *each one* in order to avoid the masculine reference, even though it is not grammatically correct:

Sexist	Each author of the Pre-Raphaelite period produced his best work prior to 1865.
Colloquial	Each author of the Pre-Raphaelite period produced their best work prior to 1865.
Formal	Authors of the Pre-Raphaelite period produced their best works prior to 1865.

Use pronouns denoting gender only when necessary to specify gender or when gender has been previously established. Avoid *man and wife* or *7 men and 16 females.* Keep them parallel by saying *husband and wife* or *man and woman* and *7 males and 16 females.*

Avoid the use of second person in research writing.

Ethnic identity

Some persons prefer the term *Black* and others prefer *African American*. The terms *Negro* and *Afro-American* are now dated and not appropriate. Use *Black* and *White*, not lowercase *black* and *white*. Some individuals may prefer *Hispanic*, *Latino*, or *Chicano*. Use the term *Asian* or *Asian American* rather than *Oriental*. *Native American* is a broad term that includes Samoans, Hawaiians, and American Indians. A good rule of thumb is to use a person's nation of origin when it is known (e.g., *Mexican*, *Korean*, or *Nigerian*).

Disability

In general, place people first, not their disability. Rather than *disabled person* or *retarded child*, say *person who has scoliosis* or *a child with Down's syndrome*. Avoid saying *a challenged person* or *a special child* in favor of *a person with* _____ or *a child with* _____. Remember that a *disability* is a physical quality while a *handicap* is a limitation that might be imposed by non-physical factors, such as a set of stairs, poverty, or social attitudes.

Editing with an eye for the inadvertent bias should serve to tighten up the expression of your ideas.

11e Participating in a Peer Review

Part of the revision process for many writers, both students and professionals, is peer review. Peer review involves giving your manuscript to a friend or classmate and asking for their opinions and suggestions. In turn, you may be asked to review your classmate's research project. You can learn by reviewing as well as by writing.

Since this task asks you to make evaluations, you need a set of criteria. Your instructor may supply a peer review sheet, or you can use the following list of suggestions. Scrutinize the paper constructively on each point. Make suggestions, offer tips, and be a help to your classmate.

Peer Review Checklist

- ◆ Does the title describe clearly what the classmate has put in the body of the paper?

- ◆ Are the subject and main issues introduced clearly?

- ◆ Is the writer's critical approach to the problem stated clearly in a thesis statement? Is it placed effectively in the introduction?

- ◆ Do the paragraphs of the body have individual unity by explaining only one idea?

- ◆ Does each paragraph relate to the thesis?

- ◆ Are sources introduced, usually with the name of the expert, and then cited by a page number within parentheses? Keep in mind that most Internet sources will not have page numbers.

- ◆ Are the sources relevant to the argument?

- ◆ Does the writer weave quotations into the text effectively while avoiding long quotations?

- ◆ Is it clear where a paraphrase begins and where it ends?

◆ Does the conclusion arrive at a resolution about the central issue?

11f Proofreading the Final Manuscript

After you have edited the text to your satisfaction or participated in a peer review, print a copy of the manuscript. Check for double spacing, one-inch margins, running heads with page numbers, and other elements. Even if you used available software programs to check your spelling, grammar, and style, you must nevertheless proofread this final version.

Proofreading Checklist

◆ Check for errors in sentence structure, spelling, and punctuation.

◆ Check for hyphenation and word division. Remember that no words should be hyphenated at the ends of lines. If you are using a computer, turn off the automatic hyphenation.

◆ Read each quotation for accuracy of your own wording and of the words within your quoted materials. Look, too, for your correct use of quotation marks.

◆ Double-check in-text citations to be certain that each one is correct and that each source is listed on your Works Cited page at the end of the paper.

◆ Double-check the format of the title page, margins, spacing, content notes, and other elements.

11g Model Research Paper in MLA Style

Cynthia Singletary
Mrs. Cohen
11th Grade English
4 May 2001

Artificial Values at the "A & P"

John Updike's short story "A & P" focuses on a young
grocery clerk named Sammy who feels trapped by the
artificial values of the small town where he lives. Sammy
describes the store and its customers as evidence to this
artificiality: "records at discount of the Carribbean Six or
Tony Martin Sings or such gunk you wonder they waste
the wax on . . . and plastic toys done up in cellophane
that fall apart when a kid looks at them anyway" (Updike
1088).[1] Sammy observes the customers daily and
proclaims them to be "houseslaves in pin curlers" (1087),
thereby suggesting that all customers are stereotypes who
no longer care about their appearances. This attitude,
according to Gilbert Porter, reveals "that implicit set of
values which will ultimately set him against community
mores" (1155). In effect, the A & P store serves as "the
common denominator of the middle-class suburbia, an
appropriate symbol for the mass ethic of a consumer-
conditioned society" (Porter 1155).

Through his perceptive eye, John Updike is "a gentle
satirist, poking fun at American life and customs"
(Liukkonen). Sammy looks at these people and sees,
through them, his own future if he allows himself to be
subjected to society's rules of conformity.

[1] Future citations to the story will be to page numbers only.

In throwing off the bonds of conformity, Sammy takes all responsibility for his actions onto himself, and in so doing he sells his innocence for freedom, a fair trade-off in the rites of passage from child to adult.

In his peculiar fashion, Sammy questions the decency of everyone else in the supermarket, referring to them as dehumanized "sheep." Sammy shows his contempt for artificiality as he comments, "I bet you could set off dynamite in an A & P and the people would by and large keep reaching and checking oatmeal off their lists . . ." (1087). Therefore, when three girls come into the A & P wearing only bathing suits and looking natural, Sammy perceives them to be the only decent things in the entire store. He becomes particularly offended when Lengel, the store manager, criticizes the girls for indecency. Sammy believes the girls are only out of place in the A & P because of its "fluorescent lights," "stacked packages," and "checkerboard green-and-cream-rubber-tile floor," all artificial things.

Lengel is the voice of the community. He manages the store in a conservative routine. For him, the girls pose a disturbance to his store, so he expresses his displeasure of their attire by reminding them that the A & P is not the beach (1088). "Decently dressed" to a man like Lengel means that girls must dress in apparel that will not draw attention. Calling attention to oneself should be reserved for the beach, not the middle of town in front of "two banks and the Congregational church and the newspaper store and three real estate offices and about twenty-seven old freeloaders tearing up Central Street because the sewer broke again" (1087). For Lengel, the appearance of indiscreet, alluring women "invokes the bawdy" (Freeman G-8). The manager prefers customers who are like sheep, which are routine animals that never stray from the herd and in times of crisis crowd together as a futile means of survival. In contrast, the entrance of the three girls is a refreshing breath that blows away Sammy's mood of oppression. He refers to them as "my girls" (1089) and labels one of them as "Queenie" to represent that she is the Queen Bee whom others follow. This Queen Bee floats across the cold tile floor on bare feet with "exceptional power and beauty" (Roberts 27). She is special as a member of a higher social class because there are few leaders and many followers in our society.

The eventual confrontation of Sammy and Lengel serves as the climax of the story. Sammy grows angry because Lengel, noticing that one girl was wearing only a two-piece suit, says, "We want you decently dressed when you come in here" (1088). In a sense, John Updike is speaking to each reader, for we must consider our own beliefs and convictions about our "intellectual and moral condition" (Schwarz 124). Lengel's social condemnation angers Sammy so much that he quits; Porter labels this act as Sammy's "rejection of the A & P and the misplaced values for which it stands" (1157).

In "A & P," John Updike suggests that the easy way, a conventional conformity to routine, is not always the best way. Updike suggests that young individualists, like Queenie and Sammy, will travel rough roads ahead in their lives, yet he also suggests that a clear conscience, which results from a refusal to conform, will prove profitable in the long run of life. The world can be hard on all individuals, so Sammy is right in taking responsibility for himself and his actions.

Works Cited

Freeman, John. "Exquisite Little Eulogies: Updike Takes
    Another Look at Familiar Terrain." *DenverPost.com*
    14 Jan. 2001: G-8. 23 Apr. 2001.
    <http://www.denverpost.com/books/
    updike0114.htm>

Liukkonen, Petri. "John (Hoyer) Updike." 13 Sept. 1999.
    25 Apr. 2001.
    <http://www.kirjasto.sci.fi/updike.htm>.

Porter, M. Gilbert. "John Updike's 'A & P': The
    Establishment and an Emersonian Cashier." *English
    Journal* 61 (1972): 1155–58.

Roberts, Rex. "Evaluating Updike." *Insight on the News*
    16. (2000): 26–27.

Schwarz, Benjamin. "Updike: America's Man of Letters."
    The Atlantic Monthly 286.6 (Dec. 2000): 124–125.

Updike, John. "A & P." *The Harcourt Brace Casebook
    Series in Literature.* Ed. Wendy Perkins. New York:
    Harcourt, 1998. 108–111.

CHAPTER 12

Handling Format — APA Style

You may be asked to write a paper in APA style, which is governed by *The Publication Manual of the American Psychological Association*. This style has gained wide acceptance in academic circles. APA style is used in the social sciences, and versions similar to it are used in the biological sciences, business, and the earth sciences.

You need to understand two basic ideas that govern this style. First, a paper written for the social sciences attempts to show what has been proven true by research for a narrowly defined subject, so it requires the **past tense** when you refer to a cited work. For example, you would write, *Lawler specified* or *the research of Lowe and Spinks has demonstrated*. Second, the social science community considers the **year of publication** as vital information, so they feature it immediately after any named source, like this: (Barlow & Simmons, 2001). These two primary distinctions, and others, are explained below.

12a Writing a Theoretical Paper for the Social Sciences

In the social sciences you will usually be expected to write a theoretical article that draws upon existing research to examine a topic. You will trace the development of a theory, examine a theory, or compare theories. Your analysis will examine the literature to arrive at the current thinking about topics, such as autism, criminal behavior, dysfunctional families, and learning disorders. It may:

1. identify a problem that has implications for the social community.

2. trace the development and history of the theory.

3. provide an analysis of articles that have explored the problem.

4. arrive at a judgment and discussion of the prevailing theory.

The research paper by Rodney Cowan on pages 173–177 demonstrates a theoretical approach to the problem of early release and parole of criminals. He identifies the problem as a lenient judicial system, traces the basic issues, cites several authorities on the topic, and arrives at his judgment that "criminals need to know they won't get off easy for their crimes."

12b Writing in the Proper Tense for an APA-style Paper

Verb tense is an indicator that distinguishes papers in the humanities from those in the natural and social sciences. MLA style, as shown in previous chapters, requires you to use present tense when you refer to a cited work, such as, "Cody *stipulates*" or "the work of Ellis and Milford *shows*"). In contrast, APA style requires you to use past tense or present perfect tense ("Cody stipulated" or "the work of Ellis and Milford has shown"). It therefore stipulates use of the past tense or the present perfect tense with its citations:

> Myers (2001) designed the experiment, and since that time two investigators have used the method (Thurman, 2000; Jones, 2001).

Note the verbs of this passage written in APA style:

> Television encourages reading, which in turn improves language competence. Beyond the one-time motivation of children who see a familiar television star who *requested* a library card, research *has indicated* that good programming *improved* reading and *increased* library lendings. The study by Bartow, McDaniel, and Lee *Television and the Adolescent Child confirmed* that "television in the long run encourages children to read books, a conclusion that can be reinforced by evidence from libraries, book clubs, and publishing companies" (Lancaster, 2000, p. 35). Dr. Bartow *made* this point: "Book reading comes into its own, not despite television but because of it" (qtd. in Lancaster, 2000, p. 35).

12c Using In-text Citations in APA style

APA style requires an in-text citation to the name of the author and the year of publication.

> Richard Conniff (2000) showed that one federal agency, the Bureau of Land Management, failed to protect the natural treasures of public land holdings, and Ralph Struble (2001) offered evidence that BLM serves the needs of ranchers, not the public.

Provide a page number only when you quote the exact words of a source, and *do* use *p.* or *pp.* with page numbers.

> Conniff (2000, p. 33) explained that the bureau must "figure out how to keep the land healthy while also accommodating cowpokes, strip miners, dirt bikers, birdwatchers and tree huggers, all vocal, all willing to sue for their conflicting rights."

If you do not use the author's name in your text, place the name within the parenthetical citation.

> It has been shown that the Bureau of Land Management often sacrifices wildlife and the environment to benefit miners and ranchers (Conniff, 2000; Struble, 2001).

When a work has two or more authors, use "&" in the citation only, not in the text.

> It has been reported (Wells & Morton, 2001) that toxic levels have exceeded the maximum allowed levels each year since 1983.

> Wells and Morton (2001) offered statistics on their analysis of water samples from six rivers in Appalachia and announced without reservation that "the waters are unfit for human consumption, pose dangers to swimmers, and produce contaminated fish that may cause salmonella (pp. 257-264)."

◇ **Exercise 12.1** In the (b) version of each sentence on page 162, make two corrections. Change the verb tense in references to a cited author and change the in-text citations from MLA style to APA style by filling the blank spaces of the parentheses. NOTE: Assume that the year of publication is 2000.

1a MLA style. Shirley Taggert defends the role of women reporters in men's locker rooms after sporting events, saying "reporters should not be judged by gender or denied access to athletes for interviews" (34).

1b APA style. Taggert (   ) defend____ the role of women reporters in men's locker rooms after sporting events, saying "reporters should not be judged by their gender or denied access to athletes for interviews following any athletic contest" (   ).

2a MLA style. One critic reports that Vietnam and Desert Storm had a destabilizing effect on our national psyche (Hardin 284).

2b APA style. One critic (   ) report____ that Vietnam and Desert Storm had a destabilizing effect on our national psyche.

3a MLA style. "Young people cannot be expected to go to college for the general good of mankind" (Bird 352).

3b APA style. One source (   ) has assert____ that "young people cannot be expected to go to college for the general good of mankind."

 Exercise 12.2 Decide which sentences below properly cite the following source in APA style.

The distinction between active and passive euthanasia is thought to be crucial for medical ethics. The idea is that it is permissible, at least in some cases, to withhold treatment and allow a patient to die, but it is never permissible to take any direct action designed to kill the patient.
—H.V. Jamison, 2001, p. 48

1. One source labels passive euthanasia as withholding treatment.

2. One source (Jamison, 2001) has labeled passive euthanasia as withholding treatment.

3. Jamison (2001) has distinguished passive euthanasia, "to withhold treatment," and active euthanasia, "to take any direct action designed to kill the patient" (p. 48).

4. Medical ethics has determined that it is never permissible to take any direct action designed to kill the patient (Jamison, 2001).

5. The differences between passive and active euthanasia have been determined (Jamison, 2001).

12d Preparing the Bibliography Page

Use the title "References" for your bibliography page. Alphabetize the entries and double-space throughout. Type the first line of each entry flush left, and indent succeeding lines five (5) spaces.

Book (APA style)

Nielsen, J., & Vollers, M. (2001). *Ice bound: A doctor's incredible battle for survival at the South Pole.* New York: Hyperion.

List the author's surname first with initials for given names. Next, give the year of publication within parentheses, and the title of the book underscored or italicized with only the first word of the title and any subtitle capitalized (but capitalize proper nouns). Then, list the place of publication and the publisher. In the publisher's name, omit the words

Publishing, Company, or *Inc.,* but otherwise give a full name: Harcourt Brace, Florida State University Press, Addison Wesley Longman.

Magazine (APA style)

Grielewski, D. (2001, January 1). The madness that swept Miami. *Smithsonian,* pp. 58–67.

List author, the date of publication (year, month, and the specific day for weekly and bi-monthly magazines), title of the article without quotation marks and with only the first word capitalized, name of the magazine underscored or italicized with all major words capitalized, and inclusive page numbers preceded by "p." or "pp."

Journal (APA style)

Davies, T. (2000). Confidence! It's role in the creative teaching and learning of design technology. *Journal of Technology Education,* 12, 1831.

List author, year, title of the article without quotation marks and with only the first word capitalized, name of the journal underscored or italicized and with all major words capitalized, volume number italicized, inclusive page numbers *not* preceded by "p." or "pp."

Newspaper (APA style)

Edwards, J. G. (2001, January 30). Electricity costs: Utilities seek record increases. *Las Vegas Review-Journal,* p. A1.

List author, date (year, month, and day), title of article with only first word and proper nouns capitalized, name of newspaper in capitals and underscored or italicized, and the section with all discontinuous page numbers.

Encyclopedia (APA style)

> Savage, W.W. "Buffalo Bill." (2000). *World book encyclopedia.* Chicago: World Book.

List author (if available), title of the article, year of the edition used, title of the encyclopedia underscored or italicized, place, and publisher.

Part of a book (APA style)

> Saltzman, J. (2000). Instant communications across cyberspace. In S.A. Kallen (Ed.), *The 1990's* (pp. 151–155). San Diego: Greenhaven.

List author(s), date, chapter or section title, editor (with name in normal order) preceded by "In" and followed by "(Ed.)" or "(Eds.)," the name of the book underscored or italicized, page numbers to the specific section of the book cited, place of publication, and publisher.

Textbook, casebook, anthology (APA style)

Make a primary reference to the anthology:

> Venner, C. (Ed.) (2001). *Raising the educational bar.* New York: Anderson & Armond.

Make cross-references to the primary source, in this case Venner. *Note: These entries should be mingled with all others on the reference page in alphabetical order so that a cross-reference may appear before or after the primary source. The year cited should be the date when the cited work was published, not when the Venner book was published. Such information is usually found in a headnote, footnote, or list of credits at the front or back of the anthology.*

> Baird, J. (2000). More testing? Give the kids a break. In Venner, pp. 35–43.

Fabrough, D. (1999). The interactive classroom. In Vesterman, pp. 69–77.

Slagle, G. (2000). Touching each child. In Vesterman, pp. 78–84.

Venner, Carl. (Ed.) (2001). *Raising the educational bar.* New York: Anderson & Armond.

The alternative to the style shown above is to provide a complete entry for every one of the authors cited from the casebook (in which case you do not need a separate entry to Venner):

Baird, J. (2000). More testing? Give the kids a break. In C. Venner (Ed.), (2001), *Raising the educational bar.* (pp. 35–43). New York: Anderson & Armond.

Fambrough, D. (1999). The interactive classroom. In C. Venner (Ed.), (2001), *Raising the educational bar.* (pp. 69–77). New York: Anderson & Armond.

Slagle, G. (2000). Touching each child. In C. Venner (Ed.), (2001), *Raising the educational bar.* (pp. 78–84). New York: Anderson & Armond.

Abstract (APA style, citing from an abstract only)

Published abstract:

Eyles, S.J. & Gierasch, L.M. (2000). Multiple roles of prolyl residues in structure and folding. [Abstract] *Journal of Molecular Biology, 301, 737.*

Unpublished abstract:

Koeneman, O. (2000). The flexible nature of verb movement. Abstract of unpublished doctoral dissertation, Utrecht Institute of Linguistics.

Book with corporate author, fourth edition (APA style)

American Psychiatric Association. (2000). *Diagnostic statistical manual of mental disorders* (4th ed.). Washington, DC: Author.

Report (APA style)

Patel, K. (2001). Kirkdale high school attendance policy (KHS 10–25). Kirkdale, MS: Media Center.

Review (APA style)

Gray, P. (2001, February 12). Tales of the African-American west [Review of *Gabriel's Story*]. *Time*, p. 85.

Nonprint material (APA style)

Carter, E. (2001, August 30). Growing greens in home gardens. [Interview.] Fayetteville, GA.

McDowell, S. T. (Producer). (2001). *Pitching the curveball* [Videotape]. Orlando: Sports Network.

Cook'n Vegetarian (2000). [Computer software]. Alpine, UT: DVO Enterprises.

12e Citing Internet Sources in APA Style

When citing Internet sources in APA style on the References page, provide this information, if available:

1. Author's/editor's last name, followed by a comma, the initials, and a period

2. Year of publication, followed by a comma, then month and day for magazines and newspapers, within parenthesis, followed by a period

3. Title of the article, not within quotations and not underscored, with only the first word and proper nouns capitalized, followed by the total number of paragraphs within brackets only if that information is provided. This is also the place to describe the work within brackets, as with [Abstract] or [Letter to the editor].

4. Name of the book, journal, or complete work, underscored or italicized, if one is listed

5. Volume number, if listed, underscored or italicized

6. Page numbers only if you have that data from a printed version of the journal or magazine. If the periodical has no volume number, use "p." or "pp." before the numbers; if the journal has a volume number, omit "p." or "pp.")

7. The word *Retrieved*, followed by the date of access, followed by the source (e.g. World Wide Web or Telnet) and a colon

8. The URLs can be quite long, but you must provide the full data for other researchers to find the source.

Article from an online journal

Dow, J. (2000). External and internal approaches to emotion: Commentary on Nesse on mood. *Psychology.* 19 Nov. 2000. Retrieved March 23, 2001, from http://www.cogsci.soton.ac.uk/cgi/psyc/ newpsy?3.01

Article from a printed journal, reproduced online

Bowler, D. M. & Thommen, E. (2000). Attribution of mechanical and social causality to animated displays by children with autism. *Autism, 4,* 147–172. Retrieved March 21, 2001, from http://www.sagepub.co.uk/ journals/details/J*O192.html

Abstract

Parrott, A. C. (2000). Does cigarette smoking cause stress? [Abstract]. *American Psychologist, 55*. Retrieved October 13, 2000, from http://www.apa.org/ journals/amp/amp5410817.html

Article from a printed magazine, reproduced online

Leahy, M. (2000). Missouri's savannas and woodlands. *Missouri Conservationist, 61*. Retrieved August 30, 2000, from http://www.conservation.state.mo.us/ conmag/2000/08/l.htm

Article from an online magazine, no author listed

Benefits of electric load aggregation. (2000, May). *PMA Online Magazine*. Retrieved March 3, 2001, from http://www.retailenergy.com/articles/loadagg.htm

Article from an online newspaper

Gallagher, S. (2000, August 11). Fires in west imperil ancient sites. *Atlanta Journal-Constitution Online*. Retrieved August 11, 2000, from http://www.accessatlanta.com/partners/ajc/ epaper/editions/today/

Bulletins and government documents

Murphy, F. L., M.D. (2000). The beneficial effects of fish oil on coronary heart disease. Preventive Health Center. Retrieved October 19, 2000, from http://www.mdphc.com/ nutrition/beneficial-effects-of-fish-oil.htm

Hypernews posting

Forster, A. (2000, May 18). The best paper of all. Recycling Discussion Group. Retrieved November 5, 2000, from http://www.betterworld.com/BvvDiscuss/get/ recycleD/26.html

Listserv (e-mail discussion group)

Fitzpatrick, B.T. (2000, November 5). Narrative bibliography. Retrieved November 8, 2000, from e-mail:bryanfitzpatrick@mail.csu.edu

Newsgroups

Haas, H. (2000, August 5). Link checker that works with cold fusion. Fogo archives. Retrieved April 25, 2000, from Usenet: impressive.net/archives/fogo/200000805113615.AI4381@w3.org

FTP site

Kranidiotis, A. A. (1994, June 7). Human audio perception frequently asked questions. Retrieved March 11, 1997, from FTP:svrftp.eng.cam.ac.uk/pub/comp.speech/info/HumanAudioPerception

12f Citing CD-ROM Information in APA Style

Material from a CD-ROM requires a distinctive citation as shown in the following examples.

Abstract

Figueredo, A. J., & McCloskey, L. A. (1993). Sex, money, and paternity: The evolutionary psychology of domestic violence [CD-ROM]. *Ethnology and Sociobiology, 14,* 353–79. Abstract from Silverplatter File: *PsychINFO* item: 81-3654.

Encyclopedia article

African American history: Abolitionist movement [CD-ROM]. (2000). *Encarta encyclopedia.* Redmond, WA: Microsoft Corporation.

Full-text article

Firestone, D. (2000, August 10). The south comes of age on religion and politics [CD-ROM]. *New York Times*, p. A-17. Article from UMI-ProQuest file: *New York Times Online*. Item 3602-108.

 Exercise 12.3 Write the following bibliograpic references in APA style.

Book:

James Lawrence, Lawrence Shulman, and William G. Bowen, *The Game of Life*. Princeton, NJ: Princeton University Press, 2000.

Magazine:

Rick Gore, "Ancient Ashkelon: Dead Men Do Tell Tales," *National Geographic*, January 2001, pages 66–90.

Journal:

Andrew J. Fuligni, Jacquelynne S. Eccles, Bonnie L. Barber, and Peggy Clements. "Early Adolescent Peer Orientation and Adjustment During High School." *Developmental Psychology*, 2001, Vol. 31, No. 1, pages 28–36.

Newspaper:

Steve Foss, "Water Quality: Experts Grapple with EPA Mandate," *Grand Forks Herald*, January 31, 2001, page 1A.

Part of a book:

"Censorship is Harmful," by Salmon Rushdie & Jonathan Rauch, chapter 1 of *Censorship*, edited by David Bender & Bruno Leone, 1997, San Diego, Greenhaven Press.

12g Formatting a Paper in APA Style

Place your materials in this order:

1. Title page

2. Abstract

3. Introduction, Body, Conclusion

4. References

5. Appendix

Title page

In addition to your title, name, and academic affiliation, the title page should establish your running head that will appear on every page preceding the page number. See page 173 for an example of a title page in APA style.

Abstract

You should provide an abstract with every paper written in APA style. An abstract is a quick but thorough summary of the contents of your paper. It is read first and may be the only part that will be read, so it must be accurate, self-contained, concise, non-evaluative, and coherent. The abstract should include:

The topic in one sentence, if possible

The purpose, thesis, and scope of the paper

A brief reference to the sources used (e.g., published articles, books, personal observation)

The conclusions and the implications of the study

Text of the paper

Double-space throughout your entire paper. In general, you *should* use subtitles as side heads and centered heads in your paper.

References

Prepare your list of references according to the designs shown in Section 12d. Present the entries with a hanging indention, as shown in Section 12d and the References section of the Sample Paper on page 177.

Appendix

The appendix is the appropriate place for material that is not relevant to your text but has pertinence to the study. You can use the appendix to present graphs, charts, study plans, observation and test results, and other matter that will help your reader understand the nature of your work.

12h Model Research Paper in APA Style

Free Crime?

Rodney Cowan
Northeast High School
March 22, 2001

Running Head: Crime

Abstract

The lenient and careless action of our judicial system is endangering the lives of every citizen. Instead of enforcing stricter and more absolute jail terms, the "system" has decided to allow criminals to be eligible for parole after increasingly shorter jail terms. This lax attitude among judges and lawyers is a slap in the face of hard-working law officers. The key to regaining our cities and helping all citizens to feel safe is to abolish parole and the early release of prisoners. The judicial system needs to give criminals longer prison terms.

Free Crime?

All across our country, convicted criminals are walking free when they should be serving time in prison. Because of the relaxed nature of our judicial system, criminals are being released from prison before they have served their whole sentence. What the system should be doing is abolishing parole and early release, while administering harsher penalties.

We need to back up our police officers when they arrest someone. Then, the criminals will be under lock and key for a long time.

> Cops in America are caught between the proverbial rock and a hard place. Faced with a staggering crime rate, yet fettered by a chronic lack of man-power and funding, police are expected to do more with less. The result: while we may win occasional battles, we're losing the overall war. (Peller, 1999, p. 41)

We need to have stricter sentencing for crimes committed and a court system that will enforce them. Someone who kills should get life in prison or the death penalty. We owe it to those who have been killed and to their families to mandate tougher sentences for murderers. The Survivors of Homicide Foundation (2001) seeks stringent penalties to "deal with the senseless, deliberate nature of the act that took the loved one." With the lax nature of current sentencing and parole policies, a killer can expect to get out of prison in five or six years.

The kind of senseless crime that needs stiffer penalties includes drunk drivers. These uncaring, mindless individuals need to be charged as killers. This was the point Kentucky Assistant General Paul Richwalsky Jr. argued during the trial of the drunk driver arrested for the fatal church bus crash in 1988 that took 27 lives. "Plain and simple," Richwalsky pointed out, "this is a murder case.

He killed them just as surely as if he had a gun" (Kunen, 1990, p. 52). Kunen further states that the families of the dead had hoped the trial would signal, once and for all, that "drinking on purpose and killing by accident" is just as intolerable as killing on purpose (52).

"Want to win the war on crime?" asked Roger Peller (1999). He then stated, "...let's forget about rehabilitation — and start rendering justice" (p. 41).

Another voice who has called for stringent penalties for criminals is Senator Joseph Biden. Speaking about the rights of victims, Senator Biden (2000) has expressed his belief that victims have the right to "notice of court proceedings, the right to confer with the prosecutor, and the right to information about the conviction, sentencing, imprisonment, and release of the offender" (2000). Echoing the sentiments of Senator Biden is the National Institute of Justice. In a survey of more than 1,300 victims of crime, 97 percent of the victims felt it was important to be involved in the decision to drop the case and to be informed about the defendant's release on bond (Survivors, 2001).

To end criminals getting out of jail early, we need to get rid of parole and parole boards. If a judge hands down a sentence, that criminal should serve the whole sentence and not get parole.

To abolish parole is not enough to stop criminals from getting out early. We also need to abolish early release for prisoners. Peller (1999) stated that a convicted burglar serving a five-year sentence may be out of the prison cell in less than 90 days (p. 42). There should not be any reduction of a sentence for good behavior. Criminals needs to serve their whole sentence.

The judicial system needs to get its act together by starting to give these criminals what they deserve—longer prison terms. Criminals need to know that they will have to pay for their crimes. This country needs to put criminals behind bars. The best way of doing this is by giving convicted criminals longer prison terms.

References

Biden, J. R. (2000, April 27). Statement of Senator Joseph R. Biden: A proposed victims' rights amendment. Retrieved March 15, 2001 from the World Wide Web: http://www.nvcan.org/docs/biden0400.htm

Kunen, James S. (1990, January 8) "Drunk Driver Larry Mahoney Gets 16 Years For The Kentucky Bus Crash That Claimed 27 Lives." *People Weekly,* 33, 51–53.

Peller, R. P. (1999, December). Plea from a veteran cop. *Keyland Review,* 13, 41–48.

Survivors of Homicide, Inc. (2001) Resources — surviving. Retrieved March 15, 2001 from http://www.survivorsofhomicide.com/ resources_-_surviving.htm

APPENDIX

Matters of Mechanics

Abbreviations Employ abbreviations often and consistently in notes and citations but avoid them in the text. In documentation, abbreviate dates (Jan. or Dec.), institutions (acad. and assn.), names of publishers (UP for University Press), and states (SD or TN).

Accents When you quote, reproduce accents exactly as they appear in the original. Use ink if your typewriter or word processor does not support the marks.

> "La tradición clásica en españa," according to Romana, remains strong and vibrant.

Ampersand Avoid using the ampersand symbol "&" unless custom demands it, as in, "A & P." Use *and* for in-text citations in MLA style (Smith and Jones 213–14), but do use "&" in APA style references (Spenser & Wilson, 1991, p. 73).

Arabic Numerals MLA style demands Arabic numerals whenever possible: for volumes, books, parts, and chapters of works; acts, scenes, and lines of plays; cantos, stanzas, and lines of poetry. Write as Arabic numerals any numbers below 10 that cannot be spelled out in one or two words (such as $3\frac{1}{2}$ or 6.234). Numbers below 10 grouped with higher numbers should appear as Arabic numerals (such as "3 out of 42 subjects" or "lines 6 and 13" but "15 tests in three categories"). Large numbers may combine numerals and words (such as 3.5 million). For inclusive numbers that indicate a range, give the second number in full for numbers through 99: 3–5, 15–21, 70–96. **MLA style:** With three digits or more give only the last two in the second number unless more digits are needed for clarity: **98–101, 110–12, 989–1001, 1030–33, 2766–854. APA style:** With three digits or more give all numbers: **110–112, 1030–1033, 2766–2854.** Spell out the initial number that begins a sentence, such as, "Thirty people participated in the initial test."

Bible Use parenthetical documentation for biblical references in the text—that is, place the entry within parentheses immediately after the quotation, for example, "(2 Kings 18.13)." Do not underscore or italicize titles of books of the Bible.

Capitalization Titles of books, journals, magazines, and newspapers: capitalize the first word and all principal words, but not articles, prepositions, conjunctions, and the *to* in infinitives, when these words occur in the middle of the title (for example, *The Last of the Mohicans*). Titles of articles and parts of books: capitalize as for books (for example, "Appendix 2," "Writing the Final Draft"). If the first line of the poem serves as the title, reproduce it exactly as it appears in print ("anyone lived in a pretty how town").

Etc. *Et cetera* means "and so forth"; avoid using the term *et cetera*. Use the term "and so on" or "and so forth."

Foreign Languages Italicize foreign words used in an English text:

> Like his friend Olaf, he is *aut Caesar, aut nihil,* either overpowering perfection or ruin and destruction.

Do not underline quotations of a foreign language:

> Obviously, he uses it to exploit, in the words of Jean Laumon, "une admirable mine de themes poetiques."

Indenting Indent paragraphs of your text five spaces. Indent long quotations 10 spaces. The opening sentence to a quoted paragraph receives no extra indentation; however, if you quote two or more paragraphs, indent the beginning of each paragraph an extra three spaces. Indent Works Cited entries five spaces on the second and succeeding lines. Indent the first line of content footnotes five spaces. Other styles, such as APA, have different requirements.

Italics Use italics to designate titles. For typed or handwritten manuscripts use underlining.

Margins A basic one-inch margin on all sides is recommended. Place your page number one-half inch down from the top edge of the paper and one inch from the right edge. If you use your name as a running head (as in MLA style), place both name and page number on the same line, flush with the right margin (see Chapter 11). Word processing may enable you to print automatically the page numbers and the running head.

Monetary Units Spell out percentages and monetary amounts only if you can do so in no more than two words. For example, *$10* or *ten dollars.*

Numbering (Pagination) Number pages in the upper-righthand corner of the page, one-half inch down from the top edge of the paper and one inch from the right edge. Pages preceding your opening page of text require lowercase Roman numerals (ii, iii, iv). Do not type a page number on a separate title page, if you have one, but do include a page number on your opening page of text, even if you include course identification. Your last name should precede the number.

Percentages Use numerals with appropriate symbols (3%, $5.60); otherwise use numerals only when they cannot be spelled out in one or two words. For example, *one hundred percent,* but *150 percent.* In business, scientific, and technical writing that requires frequent use of percentages, write all percentages as numerals with appropriate symbols.

Short Titles in the Text Use abbreviated titles of books and articles mentioned often in the text after a first, full reference. For example, *Backgrounds to English as Language* should be shortened, after initial usage, to *Backgrounds* both in the text, notes, and in-text citations but not in the bibliographic entry.

Slang Avoid the use of slang wording. When using it in a language study, enclose in double quotation marks any words to which you direct attention. Words used as words, however, require underscoring or italicizing.

Spacing As a general rule doublespace everything—the body of the paper, all indented quotations, and all reference entries.

Titles within Titles For a title that includes another indicated by quotation marks, retain the quotation marks.

> *O. Henry's Irony in "The Gift of the Magi"*
>
> According to Jacobey, "*Great Expectations* is a novel of initiation."

Underscoring (or Italicizing) for Emphasis On occasion, you may use underscoring (or italicizing when using a computer) to emphasize certain words or phrases in a typed paper, but positioning the key word accomplishes the same purpose:

Underscoring for Emphasis:
Perhaps an answer lies in <u>preventing</u> abuse, not in makeshift remedies after the fact.

Italicizing for Emphasis:
Perhaps an answer lies in *preventing* abuse, not in makeshift remedies after the fact.

Better:
Prevention of abuse is a better answer than makeshift remedies after the fact.

Word Division Avoid dividing any word at the end of a line. Leave the line short rather than divide a word.

Index